The Morning S

Vol. 15

MW00906660

TEACHING

PROPHECY

CHRONICLES

Editor: Rick Joyner
Contributing Editors: Jack Deere, Francis Frangipane, Dudley Hall
Managing Editor: Deborah Joyner Johnson
Project Manager: Dana Zondory
Layout and Design: Dana Zondory
Copy Editors: Traci Nessler, Roger Hedgspeth, Lindsey McKay, Robin Proenneke, and Deborah Williams

The Morning Star Journal® USPS012-903 is published quarterly, 4 issues per year, by MorningStar Publications, Inc. A division of MorningStar Fellowship Church, P.O. Box 440, Wilkesboro, NC 28697. Spring 2005 issue. Periodicals postage rates paid at North Wilkesboro, NC and additional mailing offices. CPC Agreement #1472593. ISSN# 10832122

POSTMASTER: Send address corrections to *The Morning Star Journal*®, P.O. Box 440, Wilkesboro, NC 28697

Subscription rates: One year $16.95; Outside U.S. $24.95 USD.

MorningStar Publications is a non-profit organization dedicated to the promulgation of important teachings and timely prophetic messages to the church. We also attempt to promote interchange between the different streams and denominations in the body of Christ.

To receive a subscription to *The Morning Star Journal*®, send payment along with your name and address to *MorningStar Publications*, P.O. Box 440, Wilkesboro, NC 28697, (336) 651-2400 (1-800-542-0278—Credit Card Orders Only); fax (336) 651-2430. One year (4 quarterly issues) U.S. $16.95; Outside U.S. $24.95 USD. Prices are subject to change without notice.

Reprints—Photocopies of any part of the contents of this publication may be made freely. However, to re-typeset information, permission must be requested in writing from *MorningStar Publications Department*, P.O. Box 440, Wilkesboro, NC 28697

BIOS

Rick Joyner is the founder, executive director, and senior pastor of MorningStar Fellowship Church. Rick is a well-known author of more than thirty books, including, *The Torch and the Sword*, the long awaited sequel to *The Final Quest* and *The Call*, and his latest, *Delivered From Evil*. He also oversees MorningStar's School of Ministry, Fellowship of Ministries, and Fellowship of Churches. Rick and his wife, Julie, live in North Carolina with their five children: Anna, Aaryn, Amber, Ben, and Sam.

Larry Randolph comes from a long line of preachers and began ministering when he was five years old. At age twenty-one, he had a dramatic encounter with the Holy Spirit which launched him into a global prophetic ministry. Larry's strong prophetic gift combined with a practical and humorous style of teaching has given many people a fresh perspective of their destiny. His strong teaching anointing enables him to make complex spiritual truths understandable. Larry is the author of *Spirit Talk* and the widely acclaimed book, *User Friendly Prophecy*.

Matt Peterson is the director of the MorningStar School of Ministry located at our H.I.M. facilities near Charlotte and the pastor of the MorningStar Fellowship Church in Winston-Salem, North Carolina. Matt and his wife, Debbie, have five sons: Josiah, Seth, Sam, John, and Andrew.

Deborah Joyner Johnson is the managing editor of the Publications Department and oversees all publishing projects for MorningStar Publications and Ministries. She shares with her brother, Rick Joyner, a desire to see the body of Christ provided with the highest quality spiritual food that is relevant for our times. Deborah's second book, *Pathway to Purpose*, was recently released through MorningStar. She has a gifted teaching ministry and shares at conferences and women's groups. Deborah lives in North Carolina and has three children: Matthew, Meredith, and Abby.

Robin McMillan is currently pastoring the MorningStar Fellowship Church at our H.I.M. facilities near Charlotte, North Carolina. With a unique preaching style, prophetic giftings, and a desire for the release of God's power, many are impacted by Robin's ministry. Robin and his wife, Donna, live in North Carolina and have four children: John Mark, Christopher, Andy, and Katy.

Steve Thompson is the associate director of MorningStar Fellowship Church, and he oversees the prophetic ministries for all of the MorningStar Fellowships. A gifted teacher and prophetic minister, Steve travels extensively throughout the United States and abroad as a conference speaker. Steve's newest book, *A 20th Century Apostle, The Life of Alfred Garr,* was released through MorningStar. Steve and his wife, Angie, reside in North Carolina with their five children: Jon, Josh, Madison, Moriah, and Olivia.

Harry R. Jackson, Jr. pastors Hope Christian Church, a 3,000-member congregation in the nation's Capitol with his wife Michele. Having earned an MBA from Harvard, Jackson ministers nationally and internationally. His writing is featured in periodicals such as *Charisma, Christian Parenting, Kairos, New Man,* and the *Elijah List.* Rev. Jackson has three books to date, *In-laws, Outlaws and the Functional Family, The Warrior's Heart,* and *High Impact African-American Churches.* He has appeared on the CBS Nightly News, BET, the O'Reilly Factor on Fox, CBN, and TBN. His articles have been featured in the *Washington Times* and the *New York Sun.*

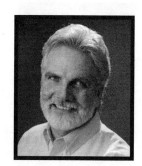

John Paul Jackson is the founder and chairman of Streams Ministries International located in North Sutton, New Hampshire. A popular teacher and conference speaker, John Paul travels around the world teaching on prophetic gifts, dreams, visions, and the realm of the supernatural. His newest publication, *Moments With God Dream Journal,* offers a unique approach to dream recording. To order his books and tapes, please call 1-888-441-8080, or visit his website at www.streamsministries.com.

Randal Cutter is the pastor of New Dawn Community Church in Coral Springs, Florida. He is a member of the MorningStar Fellowship of Ministries and his congregation is a part of the MorningStar Fellowship of Churches. Randy is an able teacher and has traveled in the United States, Britain, and the former Soviet Block releasing God's people in prophetic and healing gifts. Randy and his wife, Dawn, live in South Florida with their three children: Alyssa, Linea, and Joshua.

BIOS

John Hansen is the accounting manager for MorningStar Fellowship Church. As a former pastor, educator, and financial analyst, it is his heart to help equip people for their church or marketplace callings. John also graduated from the MorningStar School of Ministry, and resides in North Carolina with his wife Lisa and daughter Moriah.

Lilo Keller and her husband Geri lead the ministry of "Stiftung Schleife" and "Schleife Publications." For more than twenty years, they have pastored several churches in Switzerland and one in Germany. Their ministry mandate is to equip the saints by hosting conferences and seminars, as well as providing prayer and counseling opportunities for leaders and pastors. Lilo, along with her worship team, the "Reithalle Band," travel internationally. As a prophetically gifted songwriter and worship leader, she has produced nine CDs, including her piano solo production *Humming Bird* that was birthed on a sabbatical in Moravian Falls, North Carolina. Lilo has recently taken on the executive leadership of the ministry. She and Geri have two sons who are married.

Francis Frangipane is the senior pastor of River of Life Ministries in Cedar Rapids, Iowa, and the president of Advancing Church Ministries. The Lord has used Francis to unite thousands of pastors in prayer in hundreds of cities. With more than a million copies of his best selling books in print, and with an expanding radio and television ministry called "In Christ's Image," Francis is in much demand worldwide. His newest book is entitled, *It's Time to End Church Splits.*

Suzanne Hirt moved from Osteen, Florida to Charlotte, North Carolina to attend the MorningStar of School of Ministry in the fall of 2003. She is now in her second year, interning under Brad McClendon, pastor of MorningStar Fellowship in Wilkesboro. Her passion is to minister healing and deliverance to troubled youth around the world. Suzanne is currently on staff at MorningStar Fellowship Church in Wilkesboro.

Understanding the LANGUAGE OF HEAVEN

by Rick Joyner

All Christians should know the voice of the Lord. The Lord referred to Himself as **"the good shepherd" (John 10:11)** and He said in John 10:4, **"when he puts forth all his own, he goes before them, and the sheep follow him because they know his voice."** One might deduce from this that we will follow Him to the degree we know His voice. However, there can be a difference between knowing the voice of the Lord and understanding what He is saying.

For example, my wife can speak French which I do not understand. When she speaks French, I may know it is her speaking because I know her voice, but I still do not understand what she is saying. In this same way, many who know the Lord's voice misunderstand what He is saying because they do not understand the language of heaven. This is the cause of many mistakes that people make in trying to follow His guidance or understanding prophecy, including biblical prophecy.

Why Doesn't He Use Plain English?

We may wonder why the Lord does not just always speak to us in our own earthly languages so that there can be no mistakes about what He is saying. He has good reasons for not doing this. We can be sure that He does not speak to us in the language of heaven in order to confuse us. In fact, the opposite is true. He speaks to us in the language of heaven because He is trying to teach us His language, which is far more expressive, accurate, and powerful than any human language. The language of heaven will actually cut through the confusion of earthly languages so that we may all understand in unity what He is saying to us.

Even so, in our spiritual immaturity the Lord will relate and speak to us on our level. But, as we mature spiritually, He does expect us to learn to communicate spiritually. As the apostle Paul stated in I Corinthians 2:12-13:

> **Now we have received, not the spirit of the world, but the Spirit who is from God, that we might know the things freely given to us by God,**
>
> **which things we also speak, not in words taught by human wisdom, but in those taught by the Spirit, combining spiritual thoughts with spiritual words.**

AS WE MATURE SPIRITUALLY, HE DOES EXPECT US TO LEARN TO COMMUNICATE SPIRITUALLY.

This is more than just using Christian terminology. We must have a basic goal to know His voice, but also understand His language—**"spiritual words"** as Paul put it. This language does not require human intellectual brilliance as much as the heart to know the Lord and His ways. It is similar to what many people learn from being in a foreign country where they do not know the language. To begin to understand the language, you must first try to discern what the person is talking about.

For example, if I know they are talking about food, it becomes easier to recognize the words that mean certain foods. When I am in a Christian service, I usually quickly pick up the words for the Holy Spirit, Christ, etc. Then I gradually pick up the meaning of other words by their relationship to these words. So, first discerning the subject can greatly help to understand the words. The same is true in understanding the language of heaven.

However, there is another major factor that we must consider when studying the language of heaven. It is spiritual and fundamentally different from any human language. This is why in the verses that continue after those quoted above, Paul goes on to write:

> **But a natural man does not accept the things of the Spirit of God; for they are foolishness to him, and he cannot understand them, because they are spiritually appraised.**
>
> **But he who is spiritual appraises all things, yet he himself is appraised by no man.**
>
> **For who has known the mind of the Lord, that he should instruct Him? But we have the mind of Christ (I Corinthians 2:14-16).**

Some at this point may say this is too complicated and want to give up. Actually, it is more simple to understand than any human language, but it is profoundly different. It is a language more of the heart than of the mind. To understand what the Lord is really saying we must be in unity with Him. It is the same principle that the Lord spoke about in John 7:17 concerning His teaching: **"If any man is willing to do His will, he shall know of the teaching, whether it is of God, or whether I speak from Myself."** To understand His teaching, we must be willing to do His will. To understand His words, we must have His mind or be in unity with Him.

> **GETTING TO KNOW THE LORD IS THE MOST IMPORTANT FACTOR IN UNDERSTANDING HIS LANGUAGE.**

So the first principle in knowing the language of heaven is knowing the Lord and becoming unified with Him and His purposes. Because I have been married for twenty-seven years, I know exactly what my wife is going to say about something before she even speaks. This is how we must come to know the Lord.

The language of heaven is primarily what the Lord uses in prophetic dreams and visions. Interpreting dreams and visions is far more than just understanding symbolism. If it were just a matter of symbolism, it would be easy to write a computer program that could interpret any dream or vision. But such reliance on what is in fact a science in place of the Holy Spirit will almost always mislead us.

Principle #1—Know the Subject

So getting to know the Lord is the most important factor in understanding His language. That is even more fundamental than knowing the subject that He is speaking to us about. However, these two factors really go together. Most of us know people who seem to have one overriding truth on their hearts and sooner or later they are going to try to draw every conversation around to that truth. This can be boring and troublesome for some, but it is also good to be so passionate about a truth. Not that the Lord is ever boring or troublesome in the way some can be who are like this, but there are some very basic issues that are the deepest passion of His heart. They are an underlying theme to almost everything He communicates to us. The most basic of these is found in Ephesians 1:9-10:

> **He made known to us the mystery of His will, according to His kind intention which He purposed in Him**
>
> **with a view to an administration suitable to the fullness of**

the times, that is, the summing up of all things in Christ, things in the heavens and things upon the earth...

> IN EVERYTHING THE LORD IS DOING ON THE EARTH, THE ULTIMATE PURPOSE IS TO BE CONFORMED TO THE IMAGE OF CHRIST.

The ultimate purpose of God is to sum up all things in His Son. In everything the Lord is doing on the earth, the ultimate purpose is to be conformed to the image of Christ. The basic purpose for everything that is presently happening in our lives is to likewise conform us to His image. Therefore, the basis of what He is saying to us is that we must be found in Him. This is why the Lord Jesus is even called **"the Word" (John 1:1).** He is the most basic communication of God to us, which is explained further in Colossians 1:16-20:

> **For by Him all things were created, both in the heavens and on earth, visible and invisible, whether thrones or dominions or rulers or authorities—all things have been created by Him and for Him.**

> **And He is before all things, and in Him all things hold together.**

> **He is also head of the body, the church; and He is the beginning, the first-born from the dead; so that He Himself might come to have first place in everything.**

> **For it was the Father's good pleasure for all the fullness to dwell in Him,**

> **and through Him to reconcile all things to Himself, having made peace through the blood of His cross; through Him, I say, whether things on earth or things in heaven.**

Jesus is the basic Word that the Lord is speaking to us. It is for this reason that we read in Revelation 19:10, "**...For the testimony of Jesus is the spirit of prophecy.**" If someone is speaking to me in another language and I know that they are talking about a house, I can begin to understand that a certain word means "wall" and another "door" etc. Likewise, knowing that the basic communication of the Holy Spirit is about the Son, His ways, His works, and His heart, enables me to at least have a basis for beginning to interpret what the Spirit is saying.

Principle #2—It Is Not Just the Language, But How It Is Used

Though I have never learned a foreign language enough to be fluent, I always try to pick up at least some words in every foreign country in which I am traveling . I do this because even a few words in their language can help me to understand the people better. As someone once said, "Britain and America are two people divided by a common language." Even in places like Britain or Australia, where they speak English, the different phrases they use can reveal a lot about a very different way of thinking. This can be important when ministering to people, but far more important in our relationship to God. The ways He speaks to us says a lot about Him.

> **THE FATHER LOVES HIS SON ABOVE ALL THINGS, AND IS LOOKING FOR HIS SON IN ALL THINGS, INCLUDING US.**

For example, throughout the Scriptures it is obvious that the Lord loves parables. Jesus taught through parables almost exclusively. He loves to draw us after Him with mysteries that we have to search out. He is a God who likes to be pursued. Those who pursue Him will find Him. This is probably because what we spend the most time pursuing is really what we care the most about. If He really is our first love, He will be the primary pursuit of our life. We may feel obligated to obey God, but if

we are not in pursuit of knowing Him, we really may not love Him.

We can also deduce from the Scriptures that the Lord is very visual. A primary way that He has spoken to His people from the beginning is through dreams and visions. Dreams and visions are pictures. His tabernacle and temple were all filled with symbolism that was both profoundly meaningful, as well as beautiful. He loves beauty, but it is beauty with a purpose, and that purpose always points in some way to His Son. The Father loves His Son above all things and is looking for His Son in all things, including us.

The First Key to Understanding the Book of Revelation

Now let's look at how some of this applies to understanding the most prophetic book in the Bible, the book of Revelation. It is filled with mystifying symbolism and is also probably the most misunderstood book in the Bible. The primary reason for this is that most who try to tackle the meaning of its symbolism fail to understand the very first verse, especially the first five words of this verse. These verses give us the key to what He is talking about through the entire revelation—it is **"The Revelation of Jesus Christ..." (Revelation 1:1).** We will never understand this book unless we keep the first principle first, and that is, it is a revelation of Jesus above all things.

I am probably asked to speak about prophetic ministry more than any other subject. Most people are interested in the prophetic ministry in order to foretell the future or have divine insight into current events. That is a part of the prophetic, but it is not the most important or even the most interesting part. There is nothing in all of creation more interesting than God Himself. When we truly begin to behold Him, even the greatest human or earthly events cannot help but to lose their attraction. Prophetically foreseeing the future accurately is going to become increasingly important as we approach the changing of the age, but that is our duty, not our passion.

As my friend Peter Lord likes to say, "The main thing is to keep the main thing the main thing." If we know the Lord and are following Him, we will be in the right place doing the right thing regardless of whether we know what is going to happen or not. If we know the events that are coming, but are not closely following Him, then our knowledge may not do us much good.

The Second Key to the Book of Revelation

Of course the book of Revelation does include a sequence of events, which this first verse also establishes, "...the things which must shortly take place..." However, it is shocking how many seem to overlook this second key, again established in the first verse that these events were things which were to "shortly take place." The Word of God is true, and these events began to unfold very shortly after they were given to John. With remarkable accuracy, this vision foretold the unfolding of the history of the church age. One has to be almost completely ignorant of history not to see this, which is precisely the state

of much of the church—almost completely ignorant of history.

This is another fundamental reason why very few seem to ever learn the language of heaven. The greatest tool that we have in understanding the language of heaven is the Bible, God's heavenly language in written Word. It may be an English Bible or a German Bible, but those are not the real languages. If you just try to understand what is being said in English or German, you will miss a considerable part of the message.

> **PROPHETICALLY FORESEEING THE FUTURE ACCURATELY IS GOING TO BECOME INCREASINGLY IMPORTANT AS WE APPROACH THE CHANGING OF THE AGE...**

This is not to overly spiritualize the Scriptures, which has proven to be a dangerous endeavor. However, it is a language of the heart more than just a language of the mind.

The Bible is also very basically a history book. The Lord uses history to teach us His ways of dealing with men more than any other thing. Even the prophetic symbolism He uses is firmly established in history—the history of the way He has previously dealt with His people. The very word "history" was derived from the words *His-story*.

Even though the prophecies of the book of Revelation did quickly begin to unfold, and have continued to since that time, there are still some prophecies in the book of Revelation that are yet to be fulfilled. However, the works of the most popular eschatologists of the last two hundred years begins with a false assumption—that the book of Revelation deals with the future. As stated, it does still have prophecies that are yet to be fulfilled, but the majority of the book of Revelation now deals with the past more than the future, just as the very first verse indicates. If your foundation is not level when you begin to build a tower, the higher you go the more tilted it will be. The failure to understand history has caused many to build an understanding of this book on a foundation that could be easily toppled because it is so out of plumb.

How something this obvious can be so overlooked as this statement in the very first verse of Revelation is astonishing. Understanding how this has happened can help us to avoid many tragic mistakes in the future, so I do want to briefly address what I have concluded as a main reason for this is.

Because these studies so quickly lose their moorings, they inevitably seem to quickly fall into wild speculations about what the symbolism means and how they link to other biblical prophecies. By this they try to use what are in fact scientific methods without complying to even basic scientific disciplines for establishing their suppositions. This leads to conclusions that may be confidently asserted, but are really just hanging in the air with no real basis. Or worse, they make links to other Scriptures and prophecies which are fabricated or bent in order to make them fit when they really do not.

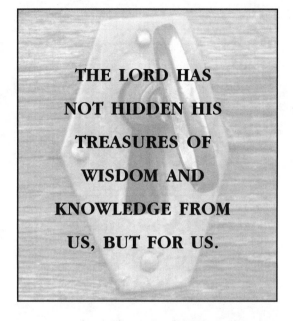

THE LORD HAS NOT HIDDEN HIS TREASURES OF WISDOM AND KNOWLEDGE FROM US, BUT FOR US.

One reason for this may be intellectual laziness. I can understand: Who wants to study history? It can be difficult and tedious, but that is the nature of treasure hunting. The Lord has not hidden His treasures of wisdom and knowledge from us, but for us. This separates those who really are not in pursuit of Him, those who would misuse the treasures if they found them. Those who do not care enough about knowing His ways to pursue understanding like treasure will remain ignorant of His ways, and usually fall into some form of deception, the very worst of which is lukewarmness.

Also, there is another key to knowledge which seems very important to the Lord. He is obviously very concerned that we honor our fathers and mothers. This is actually the only commandment that

He gave with a promise attached to it. It is repeated several times in the New Testament to assert that it is still very important to the Lord. What could be more dishonoring to our fathers and mothers than forgetting them? Therefore many of the keys to understanding the Lord, His ways, and His language are found in studying His dealings with our spiritual fathers and mothers.

> **THE LORD HAS MADE KNOWING AND UNDERSTANDING HISTORY COMPULSORY TO UNDERSTANDING PROPHECY.**

One of the significant, common denominators found with the biblical prophets is their amazing knowledge of history. The second most revealing characteristic may be their knowledge of current events. This is even more remarkable knowing that they did not have the Internet, Fox News, or even libraries to go to. The prophets were obviously very diligent to pursue this knowledge. Possibly the greatest distinguishing characteristic between those we consider "major" or "minor" prophets is the span of their basic knowledge upon which the Lord was able to impart a correspondingly broad vision.

Because studying history is a way we honor our fathers and mothers, the Lord has made knowing and understanding history compulsory to understanding prophecy. This is why the basic goal of *The Morning Star Journal* is to promote a prophetic vision moored to sound biblical doctrine, with a historical perspective. These are three cords that together cannot be easily broken.

The Third Key to the Book of Revelation

The third main key to understanding the language of heaven is to understand God's basic purpose in restoration. As we read previously in Colossians, the basic purpose of God was to make all things through His Son, for Him, and that in Him all things would hold together. We were originally made in His image. Because this image was marred by the Fall, we must understand God's heart for restoration. He is going to fully restore man to the image of His Son, and all things to their original purpose, as we read in Acts 3:19-21:

> **Repent therefore and return, that your sins may be wiped away, in order that times of refreshing may come from the presence of the Lord;**
>
> **and that He may send Jesus, the Christ appointed for you,**
>
> **whom heaven must receive until the period of *restoration of all things* about which God spoke by the mouth of His holy prophets from ancient time.**

Here we see that it is a part of God's ultimate intention to "restore all things."

This includes all things which need restoration, all that were lost by the Fall. To understand His language we must understand what He is trying to say to us, and restoration is one of His basic messages.

Likewise, if we are going to be His messengers, we must have a heart for the things that are on His heart. The prophetic heart is one that is in union with God's heart. Prophetic eyes are eyes that see what He sees. Therefore, the goal of all prophetic ministry should be to be in union with Him. At the very basis of all that God does is redemption and reconciliation so that the ultimate goal of restoration can be accomplished. The first thing He is seeking to restore is His image in His people, and then through His people to all people. Then He will, through man to whom He gave authority over the earth, restore the earth which was corrupted through man's fall.

Summary

Because restoration is such an expansive subject which is especially relevant to the gospel of the kingdom that is to be preached at the end of this age and has become a greatly misunderstood and controversial subject, I will devote an entire article just to that subject in the next edition of *The Morning Star Journal*. I will take some time also to examine some of the extremes and distortions of this that have made it so controversial. Even so, as we will see, God's heart for restoration is one of the most profound revelations of His heart and His glory. It is also the fundamental purpose of His kingdom. One reason the gospel of the kingdom has not yet been preached is the failure to perceive His heart for restoration. When we do see this we will not be able to keep from preaching the glorious gospel of His kingdom!

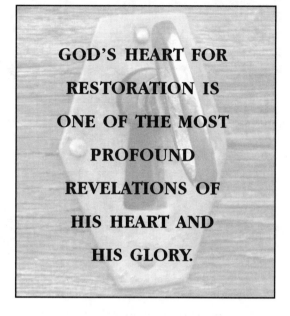

GOD'S HEART FOR RESTORATION IS ONE OF THE MOST PROFOUND REVELATIONS OF HIS HEART AND HIS GLORY.

What we have covered here are just some of the most basic principles of understanding the language of heaven. In the coming editions of *The Morning Star Journal*, we will also continue our study of the language of heaven, including interpreting dreams and visions, and the other forms of prophetic revelation. Some of this material is available now through books and teachings that we have released on the subject. However, much of it has never been taught or written before, and will be taken from many actual revelations and events that have come to us over many years of pursuing this ministry. As we come closer to the change of the age, it will become increasingly crucial for us to understand. ■

PEOPLE and Prophecy

by Larry Randolph

For no prophecy was ever made by an act of human will, but men moved by the Holy Spirit spoke from God (II Peter 1:21).

One of the fondest memories of God's intervention in my life came as a result of an inspired message given to me by an old prophet named Robert Mitchell. Before I met this prophet, I was in total confusion about the direction of my life. I had a young family, no money, a call to ministry, and a great desire to attend Bible school.

A friend who knew this dear man of God insisted that we drive to his little cottage in rural Arkansas in order to receive a prophetic word. I was reluctant at first but eventually agreed to make the trip. When we arrived, the prophet (nearly one hundred years old) greeted us at the door with a smile worthy of an angel. He graciously asked us into his house and arranged two chairs for us to sit on. What followed drastically changed the course of my life.

Before I was comfortable in my chair, this wonderful old man began to speak prophetically to me. He said, "I see a young man with a family. He has no finances. He is called to ministry and has been praying about going to Bible school."

He then leaned forward and looked deep into my eyes as if he knew everything else about my life. "Son, it's not God's will for you to go to Bible school. It is true you are called, but God wants to personally train you. What He has planned for you cannot be learned in a classroom. Soon God will open a door of ministry, and you will see His financial provision. So stand still and see the salvation of the Lord."

> ONE OF THE GREATEST CONTROVERSIES IN CHRISTENDOM HAS TO DO WITH THE ISSUE OF WHETHER OR NOT GOD SPEAKS THROUGH THE VOICE OF PROPHECY TODAY.

With a twinkle in his eye he continued, "Do not be disappointed. You're going to school alright, but it is going to be the school of the Holy Spirit and the school of hard knocks." Then he smiled, opened his Bible, and began to give me further instruction about other issues relating to my destiny. When he had finished, I knew I had seen a glimpse of God's will for my life.

Hardly two months passed before things began to fall in line with the prophetic word I had received. It became impossible for me to go to Bible school, and I was offered ministry at a church where I spent the next several years learning the true meaning of "on the job training." I encountered the difficulty of working a secular job, studying the Scriptures at night, and ministering at the church almost every weekend. When I did transition to full-time service, I was better equipped to fulfill an unusual ministry that I could not have prepared for in seminary. Thank God I listened to the word of the Lord through one of His servants instead of the conventional wisdom in my head.

Talking for God

One of the greatest controversies in Christendom has to do with the issue of whether or not God speaks through the voice of prophecy today. Many in the church believe it is arrogant, if not impossible for men to speak for God. Others believe it is possible but unlikely, since we are living in a dispensation of time in which they believe God speaks only through the agency of Scripture.

Regardless of either view, I am convinced that God has always talked through His people and will continue until such time that He returns to earth. In fact, He ordained scores of men and women to speak on His behalf throughout the Bible. According to II Peter 1:21, men of God spoke for the Lord as they were moved by the inspiration of the Holy Spirit. The Psalmist David confirmed this truth in II Samuel 23:2 and declared, **"The Spirit of the Lord spoke by me, and His word was on my tongue."** Zacharias also prophesied in Luke 1:70 that God has spoken through the mouth of men from the very beginning.

Other examples apply, such as the time in Genesis 20:3 when Abraham spoke the word of the Lord to King Abimelech. Moses and Aaron were, likewise, commissioned as God's spokesmen in the book of Exodus, and both David and Samuel were well-known for their ability to articulate the heart of God. For the most part, the greater part of the Old Testament is filled with the writings of men that were deputized to speak on God's behalf.

In the New Testament era, Christ's disciples were also commissioned to speak for Him. They were instructed by the Lord in Matthew 10:7 to go into the entire world and declare **"the kingdom of heaven is at hand."** Years later, they wrote about the issue of the end times in Scripture and indicated that it was a prophetic word for all to declare. In fact, Peter described the last days in Acts 2:17 as a time when our sons and daughters will proclaim the advent of God's kingdom through the voice of prophecy.

The Gift

What is prophecy? The essence of the words "prophecy and prophesy" in the Greek language means to declare, to announce, to predict, to foretell, or to speak under inspiration. In basic terms, prophecy is God speaking through man. It is simply the authoritative announcement of God's will to man and is substantiated over four hundred times in the Old Testament where men of God declared, **"Thus says the Lord."**

The New Testament is also filled with extraordinary examples of prophecy in action. The apostle Paul instructs us in I Corinthians 14:1 to **"desire spiritual gifts,"** especially the gift of prophecy. It appears that he understood the value of this gift and clarified its use throughout the remaining verses of chapter fourteen. He began by identifying prophecy as the primary means to encourage the people

of God. This is partly due to the fact that the spiritual DNA of the prophetic consists of edification, exhortation, and comfort.

In I Corinthians 14:31, Paul also addressed the issue of who can prophesy by indicating that the voice of prophecy belongs to anyone who has a heart to build-up the people of God. According to this thesis, the issue of who can prophesy is not necessarily determined by our spiritual maturity or ministry status, but by our availability and accessibility. According to Exodus 4:14, Aaron became God's spokesman, not because he was tremendously gifted, but because he was available.

IN BASIC TERMS, PROPHECY IS GOD SPEAKING THROUGH MAN.

Like many ordinary men in the Bible, we too must accept the humbling reality that God has chosen to express Himself through the frailty of mankind. The qualifying factor for that expression does not come from our performance, but from our friendship with God. Of course, prophecy is vented through the uniqueness of a person's character, voice, and language. Nevertheless, the inspiration to prophesy comes from God and is birthed out of intimacy with Him. The bottom line is: Friends tell friends secrets.

Inspiration or Opinion?

In spite of the importance of prophetic ministry today, we must never value prophecy above the Scriptures. The Bible is God's definitive voice and best reveals His intent for mankind today. This means prophecy should never contradict the Scriptures, nor should it stand apart from the witness of Scriptures.

Therefore, if someone gives you a message in the name of God that is crosscurrent to the principles found in the Bible, you are under no obligation to receive their word. It is not only your right to judge prophecy, but according to I Corinthians 14:29, it is your God-given duty. Paul clearly states in I Corinthians 2:15 that a spiritual man discerns all things that pertain to his life. This includes everything from slight impressions to prophetic words given by high level prophets.

Several years ago, I received a prophetic word from an internationally known prophet who has a reputation for accuracy. Yet, because his word was different than what God had previously revealed to me through the Scriptures, I had to put it on a shelf where it remains to this very day. I greatly respect the man's ministry and have received other prophetic words from him that have been amazingly precise. In this particular instance, however, I was forced to make the distinction between inspiration and opinion.

Does this mean I am to disrespect prophetic ministry because of one negative experience? Absolutely not! I have learned that the honest mistake of a prophetic person does not make him a false prophet any more than a wrong diagnosis by a physician makes him a false doctor. Certainly, I must guard against such mistakes, but it would be foolish to refuse further help just because they are human.

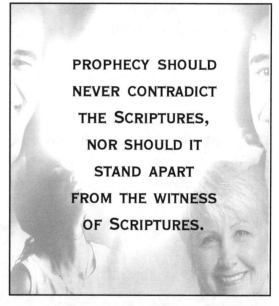

PROPHECY SHOULD NEVER CONTRADICT THE SCRIPTURES, NOR SHOULD IT STAND APART FROM THE WITNESS OF SCRIPTURES.

When all is said and done, I still receive guidance and comfort from the prophetic word spoken through the mouth of people today. In one instance, I was freed from several years of mental anguish by the words of a friend who said the Lord instructed him to tell me, "God does not hate your guts." He did not know that a voice had been telling me for over a year that God was displeased with me and hated my guts. When I heard the true word of the Lord through the mouth of my friend, the other voice left immediately and has never returned.

Highlights

Now for some highlights that will serve us in the days ahead. As I have abundantly stated, God has chosen to speak through mouths of clay. He uses extraordinary people, ordinary people, educated people, uneducated people, young people, and old people. Actually, the Lord seemed to take special delight in the Old Testament by using children such as Samuel, David, and Joseph to speak His word. He also used Anna, an eighty-four year old widow, to prophesy over the infant Christ in Luke 2:36-38.

Next, it is important to the welfare of a believer to value the gift of prophecy. It is written in II Chronicles 20:20, **"believe His prophets, and you shall prosper."** (NKJV) Paul also tells us in I Thessalonians 5:20 that we should not despise the voice of prophecy or those through whom it is spoken. In several instances in the Old Testament, Israel lost their way because they were indifferent to the word of the Lord spoken through prophetic people.

Finally, every word from God has the potential to rout our enemies. In other words, when our destiny is confirmed by prophetic utterance it has the potential to ward off any evil weapon Satan has formed to destroy our future. It is clear in I Timothy 1:18 that we can wage a good warfare according to the prophecy that has been spoken over us. ■

*This article is an excerpt from Larry's newest book, **Spirit Talk**, which is available through our website: **www.morningstarministries.org** or by calling, **1-800-542-0278**.*

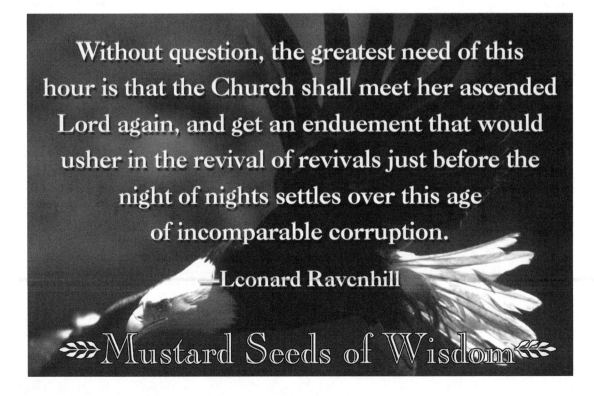

Without question, the greatest need of this hour is that the Church shall meet her ascended Lord again, and get an enduement that would usher in the revival of revivals just before the night of nights settles over this age of incomparable corruption.

—Leonard Ravenhill

Mustard Seeds of Wisdom

Trusting God

by Matt Peterson

The most important battles of our lives are not fought before crowds of thousands, they are the internal skirmishes waged in our hearts daily—the reoccurring battle between trusting in God or trusting in ourselves.

In an attempt to influence this battle, the enemy will use whatever means are at his disposal to inhibit a believer from giving God all of his or her heart and choosing to trust Him. Difficult circumstances, feelings, fears, deception, lies, intellectualism, and the seeming uncertainty of faith are all aimed at deterring us from daring to trust God. Entertaining in our minds any of the enemy's logical reasons to withhold trust in God is deadly.

A life ruled by fear and anxiety is the result of remaining a passenger in the boat of logic and reason. On the other hand, reckless trust in the One who loves us releases the power and support of God.

Revelation of Love

Throughout the history of mankind, God has been looking for people who would trust Him entirely. From Adam and Eve, to the Israelites in the wilderness, to our present lives, **"…the eyes of the LORD move to and fro throughout the earth that He may strongly support those whose heart is completely His…" (II Chronicles 16:9).**

The heart fully given over to God trusts Him with all. This magnitude of trust is rare, but it is the desire of God and His invitation to every person. The eyes of the Lord are searching, seeking among the billions of people on the earth, those through whom He can bring the resources of heaven. When His gaze reaches our heart, is it **"completely His?"**

Although God is worthy of being trusted, one of the greatest challenges in the earth is the daily choice of trusting an invisible Being with all that is precious to us. Trusting God is the radical placing of our entire being—all that belongs to us and everything that is out of our control in His care. This is a daily action—not a one-time transaction.

Trust in Him at all times, O people; pour out your heart before Him; God is a refuge for us. Selah (Psalm 62:8).

But as for me, I trust in You, O Lord,

I say, "You are my God."

My times are in Your hand… (Psalm 31:14-15).

casting all your anxiety on Him, because He cares for you (I Peter 5:7).

Knowing in our minds that we should trust God and actually making the transaction of trusting Him daily with everything in our care are two entirely different things. A believer can attend church for fifty years and have the Bible memorized, but still not trust God because trust is separate from duty and knowledge.

For us to surrender all of our hearts to anyone, we must either be completely deceived or know that we are utterly loved. Only believers who know they are unconditionally loved by God will dare to surrender all, following Him into the unknown. *Believing and experiencing the love of God paves the only road that trust dares to travel.* If there is a hint of doubt concerning God's trustworthiness, a portion of our hearts will be reserved.

This makes it absolutely critical for all believers to have a personal and ongoing revelation of God's love for them.

May the Lord direct your hearts into the love of God and into the steadfastness of Christ (II Thessalonians 3:5).

BELIEVING AND EXPERIENCING THE LOVE OF GOD PAVES THE ONLY ROAD THAT TRUST DARES TO TRAVEL.

Jesus fulfilled His purpose on the earth because He knew that His Father loved Him (see John 3:35). Similarly, as we believe that God loves us unconditionally, we will move forward in trust and faith in Him, and our purpose on the earth will also be fulfilled.

Reserving areas of our hearts will cause us to be unhealthy, confused, and cursed. Striving, confusion, and weariness result from us trying to support by our own strength what we have withheld from God.

…Cursed is the man who trusts in mankind and makes flesh his strength, and whose heart turns away from the Lord.

For he will be like a bush in the desert and will not see

when prosperity comes, but will live in stony wastes in the wilderness, A land of salt without inhabitant.

Blessed is the man who trusts in the LORD And whose trust is the LORD (Jeremiah 17:5-7).

The person who has a revelation of God's love and dares to trust Him entirely is supplied with blessing and the supernatural power and support of heaven.

Often without realizing the consequences of not trusting God, many have become enslaved, unable to see when prosperity comes. Most fears, anxieties, and financial problems exist because we do not trust in God.

He who trusts in his own heart is a fool...(Proverbs 28:26).

Erosion of Trust

From the very beginning, Satan's strategy has been to erode man's trust in God by making us suspicious of God's motives or love toward us. Satan knows that if we are suspicious of God and not fully convinced of His love, we will withhold our trust from Him and fall under a curse.

In the Garden, the serpent said to Eve: "You surely will not die! For God knows that in the day you eat from it you eyes will be opened, and you will be like God, knowing good and evil" (Genesis 3:4-5).

Satan sowed a seed in Eve's heart that was a direct attack on the character of God, causing her to doubt His love for her. By entertaining the thought that God may have been withholding His best, fear and confusion entered and Eve began to take matters into her own hands. Deceived by suspicion, Eve then tried to obtain what she believed God was withholding through her own efforts. The curse followed.

MOST FEARS, ANXIETIES, AND FINANCIAL PROBLEMS EXIST BECAUSE WE DO NOT TRUST IN GOD.

Suspicion concerning God's heart also kept an entire generation of freed Israelites from entering their promised inheritance. When the report about the Promised Land reached the ears of the people of Israel, "...you grumbled in your tents and said, 'Because the LORD hates us, He has brought us out of the land of Egypt to deliver us into the hand of the Amorites to destroy us'" (Deuteronomy 1:27).

Suspicion toward the heart of God will always deceive people into believing the exact opposite of what is true. Because Israel did not trust God, reports of the Promised Land sounded like a trap instead of an inheritance, and hatred instead of love. That entire generation lived under a curse until death because they chose to doubt God's heart toward them, even though God had shown Himself loving to them numerous times in powerful and miraculous ways. One thought of suspicion taints and attempts to nullify everything we have ever known or experienced of God previously. Suspicion is an accusation believed, and it is the enemy's primary attack against the people of God.

God's heart must have been broken as He watched His people doubt His love and choose death over life. The truth of God's heart for Israel was that "...**in the wilderness where you saw how the LORD your God carried you, just as a man carries his son, in all the way which you have walked until you came to this place. But for all this, *you did not trust the LORD your God*, who goes before you on your way, to seek out a place for you to encamp, in fire by night and cloud by day, to show you the way in which you should go.**" (Deuteronomy 1:31-33). God cared for them by providing and showing them the way they should go even while they were doubting, grumbling, and being suspicious of Him. God is love and is worthy to be trusted.

The prophet Jeremiah fought this same battle with suspicion. Recorded in Scripture is one of Jeremiah's prayers of complaint toward the Lord as he says, **"Why is my pain perpetual and my wound incurable, refusing to be healed? Will You (God) indeed be to me like a deceitful brook, like waters that fail and are uncertain?"**

Immediately, the Lord responded to his personal complaint by saying, **"Therefore thus says the Lord [to Jeremiah]: If you return [and give up this mistaken tone of distrust and despair], then I will give you again a settled place of quiet and safety, and you will be My minister; and if you separate the precious from the vile [*cleansing your own heart from unworthy and unwarranted suspicions concerning God's faithfulness*], you shall be My mouthpiece. [But do not yield to them]. Let them return to you—not you to [the people]"** (Jeremiah 15:18-19 AMP).

> SUSPICION IS AN ACCUSATION BELIEVED, AND IT IS THE ENEMY'S PRIMARY ATTACK AGAINST THE PEOPLE OF GOD.

Jeremiah was confronted with unworthy and unwarranted suspicions concerning God's faithfulness, so he had to repent before he could again be used by God as His mouthpiece.

Yielding to the enemy's suspicion toward God makes every opportunity for victory seem hopeless and appearing to be a setup for defeat. If we are suspicious of God's heart for us, we will have a warped view of Him, becoming blinded to His provision.

Today, the enemy's strategy against us will often come with questions like: "What if God will never give me someone to marry?" "What if I can't provide for my family?" "What if I get cancer?" "What if God has no place of ministry for me?" "What if I take a step of faith and it doesn't work out?" Or, "What if God is not really that good?" The realm of Satan is the realm of the "what if's," followed by something negative concerning God.

Trust is aborted by entertaining suspicion or "what if" questions in our mind. This is also one of the primary ways that people get into terrible relationships, make bad career decisions, get themselves into deep financial debt, produce detrimental ministry, and find themselves out of His will. Making life choices from a reaction to suspicion or "what if" questions keeps us enslaved.

> **Many sorrows shall be to the wicked; but he who trusts in the LORD, mercy shall surround him (Psalm 32:10 NKJV).**

God's mercy surrounds those who believe the best about His heart at all times, and choose to trust Him daily. He will take care of the rest.

Daring to Trust

Trusting God is a fight that we can and must win. Key to making the daily decision of trusting God is believing that God is good to the core and His Word is true. Standing on His Word and refusing to consider or entertain anything to the contrary is vital, regardless of how real the feeling is or how strong the negative thought may be. Jesus fought every attack from the enemy with **"It is written."** If the Word, who became flesh and dwelt among us, used the written Word to fight Satan, we must all the more.

> **GOD'S MERCY SURROUNDS THOSE WHO BELIEVE THE BEST ABOUT HIS HEART AT ALL TIMES, AND CHOOSE TO TRUST HIM DAILY.**

One aspect of taking every thought captive is to categorically reject every thought or feeling that taints our view of God's heart toward us. God loves us, has given us everything pertaining to life and godliness, will never leave or forsake us, has a plan for our lives, and has prepared good things for us that we cannot even imagine. God is worthy of and deserving of our complete trust.

Our transformation into the image of Jesus is done one battle of trust at a time. By believing the words of Christ, repenting of our suspicion, and refusing to entertain any thought that is contrary to the truth in His Word, we will be able to put our trust in Him at every turn and watch Him provide and support His will being fulfilled in our lives.

> **Commit your way to the LORD, trust also in Him, and He will do it (Psalm 37:5).** ■

DEFEATING DISCOURAGEMENT

by Deborah Joyner Johnson

Many of life's failures are people who did not realize how close they were to success when they gave up.

— Thomas Edison

When we become discouraged, it is a struggle to do much of anything, especially to fulfill a goal. *Webster's Dictionary* defines discouragement like this: "to deprive of courage, hope, or confidence; dishearten." Discouragement is the absence of courage. Without courage, we will not have the boldness to tackle even the smallest goal in life.

Discouragement is an enemy that we must fight at every turn. Discouragement cost one generation of Israelites a blessed life in the Promised Land. When God delivered them from the Egyptians, who had enslaved them for generations, He

intended for them to live a good life. Moses sent twelve men, one from each tribe, to go and spy out the Promised Land. They were pleased with the land and **"they also took some of the fruit of the land in their hands and brought it down to us; and they brought back word to us, saying, 'It is a good land which the LORD our God is giving us'"** **(Deuteronomy 1:25 NKJV).** The fruit was huge and scrumptious and the land was theirs for the taking.

But fear took their hearts when they saw the size of the men that they would have to fight to occupy the Promised Land, causing them to become discouraged. Moses was not happy with them when he heard their complaining and fear. He told them: **"and you complained** in your tents, and said, 'Because the LORD hates us, He has brought us out of the land of Egypt to deliver us into the hand of the Amorites, to destroy us. Where can we go up? Our brethren have *discouraged* our hearts, saying, 'The people are greater and taller than we; the cities are great and fortified up to heaven; moreover we have seen the sons of the Anakim there'" (emphasis mine, **Deuteronomy 1:27-28** NKJV).

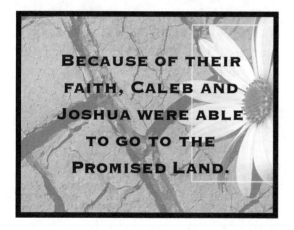

BECAUSE OF THEIR FAITH, CALEB AND JOSHUA WERE ABLE TO GO TO THE PROMISED LAND.

They became so discouraged and depressed that they were deceived into believing that the Lord hated them! Yet, He had delivered them from a horrible life in Egypt, as Moses reminded them. And, had they just had faith, He would have helped them fight the Amorites and win the battle. Moses tried to help them see the truth: "**Do not be terrified, or afraid of them. The LORD your God, who goes before you, He will fight for you, according to all He did for you in Egypt before your eyes, and in the wilderness where you saw how the LORD your God carried you, as a man carries his son, in all the way that you went until you came to this place. Yet, for all that, you did not believe the LORD your God** (**Deuteronomy 1:29-32** NKJV).

Because they allowed discouragement to grip them, fear caused them to believe they could not win this battle. They even turned on the Lord! Moses became very angry with His chosen people and told them: "**And the LORD heard the sound of your words, and was angry, and took an oath, saying, 'Surely not one of these men of this evil generation shall see that good land of which I swore to give to your fathers, except Caleb the son of Jephunneh; he shall see it, and to him and his children I am giving the land on which he walked, because he wholly followed the LORD…and Joshua the son of Nun, who stands before you he shall go in there."** (**Deuteronomy 1:34-36, 38** NKJV). Joshua and Caleb believed that they could take the land easily, but the Israelites would not listen, until it was too late. Because of their faith, Caleb and Joshua were able to go to the Promised Land. A whole generation lost out on the blessing of a wonderful life because they believed the discouraging report from men, rather than to fight and take the land that the Lord had promised them.

Fight Discouragement

Satan does not want any of us to live the kind of life we were born to live. We cannot and must not listen to his lies. Discouragement can be devastating in our lives, and we must not let it rule us; we must fight the battle he has set against us until we win. And just like the Lord would have helped the Israelites win against the Amorites, the Lord will help us win the battle.

We have all faced discouragement, and we must conquer this ongoing enemy if we are to ever succeed in fulfilling our purpose in life. Discouragement can drain the life out of us until it is a struggle to focus on anything. Galatians 6:9 gives us courage to keep going: **"So don't get tired of doing what is good. Don't get discouraged and give up, for we will reap a harvest of blessing at the appropriate time"** (NLT).

TAKE COURAGE AND FIGHT FOR YOUR DREAMS WITH ALL YOUR MIGHT.

The enemy would enjoy seeing us discouraged all the time, living meaningless lives. This, however, is not God's plan for us. We may all be familiar with the Scripture in Philippians 4:13, but do we truly believe it? **"I can do all things through Him who strengthens me."** The Lord is the One who gives us the strength to do what He has called us to do. We must never lose sight of this.

When we become discouraged, the Lord is only a prayer away, and He will help us. Just as Psalm 27:14 says: **"Wait for the LORD; be strong, and let your heart take courage; yes, wait for the LORD."** God is with us. We must have the faith to believe this. He does not want to see us discouraged in any way, for it is a sad and lonely place to be. We can triumph in the area of discouragement through faith.

Do not ever give up on your dreams. Discouragement will drain your creativity and make you think it is not worth the cost. Take courage and fight for your dreams with all your might. Every battle will be worth it in the end. Norman Vincent Peal said this well: "Stand up to your obstacles and do something about them. You will find that they haven't half the strength you think they have." Jim Valvano, N.C. State's former basketball coach, told his team: "Don't give up; don't ever give up!" With his encouragement and the team's perseverance, they won the 1983 NCAA championship!

Plow Through

Like many, I have had to fight discouragement much of my life, and I have learned many lessons in my battles. A huge lesson I have learned is to take authority over my thoughts. Let me explain. A series of events happened during one week and I was feeling discouraged; I just could not shake it. It became worse as the week progressed. Discouragement was choking the very life out of me. I knew I needed to overcome, but I could not seem to do it.

On Friday evening of that week I was working in my garden, and as I began to remove the weeds with a hoe, the thought occurred to me to plow through how I was feeling. I wondered how to do this and then I realized I should begin thanking the Lord for all of the blessings in my life. Even though I did not feel like it, I began praising Him, and before long, I found that my eyes were no longer focused on myself, but were focused on Him. As I continued to praise Him for His goodness, discouragement began to dissipate and I actually began to feel happy again. I had plowed through discouragement and had sown the exact opposite of what I was feeling. The Lord gave me the reward of joy. Hebrews 13:15 exhorts us to **"...continually offer up a sacrifice of praise to God, that is, the fruit of lips that give thanks to His name."** By offering praise to the Lord, truly thanking Him for all He has done in our lives, we will find that discouragement will not have a grip on us and it will actually leave.

You only have the time the Lord has given to you. What will you do with your time? What is it that burns within you to accomplish? Do not let the fire go out until your goals are reached! You will never be truly happy until you are doing what you were born to do. Helen Keller once said:

"Many people have a wrong idea of what constitutes true happiness. It is not attained through self-gratification, but through fidelity to a worthy purpose." Coming from a woman who was deaf and blind, this statement has amazing meaning. She accomplished far more goals in her life than most do with all of their five senses. Helen Keller learned the key to this happiness is to begin, and then to finish something that is of worth. However, you cannot finish what you do not start. ■

Take the first step in faith. You don't have to see the whole staircase, just take the first step.

—*Dr. Martin Luther King, Jr.*

❧ ❧ ❧

*This article is an excerpt from Deborah's newest book, **Pathway to Purpose**, which is available through our website: **www. morningstarministries.org** or by calling, **1-800-542-0278**.*

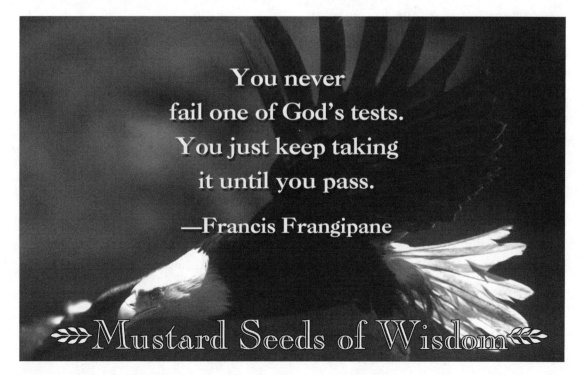

You never
fail one of God's tests.
You just keep taking
it until you pass.

—Francis Frangipane

≫ Mustard Seeds of Wisdom ≪

Accessing Heaven
Part II

All Scriptures are New King James Version unless otherwise indicated.

by Robin McMillan

The world is in desperate need of demonstrations of the supernatural power and provision of the Lord. Many of God's people yearn to walk with Him in the Spirit at this high level of experience. But how do we access this heavenly provision and make it an earthly reality?

Three valuable keys are revealed in the patriarch Jacob's initial divine encounter. First, God's availability to His people is based upon His mercy and not our deservedness. Second, our response to Him moves Him. Third, the Lord is closer to us than we know.

God Is Merciful

God revealed His mercy so abundantly in His dealings with Jacob. From birth, Jacob demonstrated his scheming nature by grabbing the heel of his twin brother Esau as he followed him out of the womb (see Genesis 25:26). Even then he sought to gain an advantage by any available means. As an adult, he exploited his brother's weakness, buying Esau's valuable birthright from him for a bowl of stew. Later, Jacob deceived his father Isaac by impersonating Esau, gaining the elder brother's blessing (see Genesis 25:29-34 and 27:8-40).

Esau was so angry that he determined to kill his brother. Jacob's mother urged Jacob to flee for his life. It was under these circumstances that God revealed Himself to Jacob in the middle of the night after he fled from home.

Now Jacob went out from Beersheba and went toward Haran.

So he came to a certain place and stayed there all night, because the sun had set. And he took one of the stones of that place and put it at his head, and he lay down in that place to sleep.

Then he dreamed, and behold, a ladder was set up on the earth, and its top reached to heaven; and there the angels of God were ascending and descending on it.

And behold, the LORD stood above it and said: "I am the LORD God of Abraham your father and the God of Isaac; the land on which you lie I will give to you and your descendants.

Also your descendants shall be as the dust of the earth; you shall spread abroad to the west and the east, to the north and the south; and in you and in your seed all the families of the earth shall be blessed.

Behold, I am with you and will keep you wherever you go, and will bring you back to this land; for I will not leave you until I have done what I have spoken to you."

Then Jacob awoke from his sleep and said, "Surely the LORD is in this place, and I did not know it."

And he was afraid and said, "How awesome is this place! This is none other than the house of God, and this is the gate of heaven!"

Then Jacob rose early in the morning, and took the stone that he had put at his head, set it up as a pillar, and poured oil on top of it.

And he called the name of that place Bethel; but the name of that city had been Luz previously.

THREE VALUABLE KEYS ARE REVEALED IN THE PATRIARCH JACOB'S INITIAL DIVINE ENCOUNTER.

Then Jacob made a vow, saying, "If God will be with me, and keep me in this way that I am going, and give me bread to eat and clothing to put on,

so that I come back to my father's house in peace, then the LORD shall be my God.

And this stone which I have set as a pillar shall be God's

house, and of all that You give me I will surely give a tenth to You (Genesis 28:10-22).

Without one hint of reproof or rebuke, God promised to help, protect, provide, and fulfill Jacob's prophetic destiny. It was not that God permanently disregarded Jacob's faults. In his future awaited another dark night by the river Jabbok where he would wrestle with God until he finally faced his own evil nature. There the Lord changed him into another kind of man. But until then God's mercy prevailed. How wonderful is our God.

Paul's Experience of Mercy

The apostle Paul describes the richness and depth of God's mercy:

But God—so rich is He in His mercy! Because of and in order to satisfy the great and wonderful and intense love with which He loved us,

Even when we were dead (slain) by [our own] shortcomings and trespasses, He made us alive together in fellowship and in union with Christ; [He gave us the very life of Christ Himself, the same new life with which He quickened Him, for] it is by grace (His favor and mercy which you did not deserve) that you are saved (delivered from judgment and made partakers of Christ's salvation) (Ephesians 2:4-5 AMP).

Paul experienced the mercy of God in a dramatic way. The Lord revealed Himself to Paul in a flashing light of glory while on the road to Damascus to imprison any Jewish Christians he could find. The Lord did so to demonstrate His mercy and establish Paul as a living example of it. Note Paul's explanation for why the Lord saved him:

However, for this reason I obtained mercy, that in me first Jesus Christ might show all longsuffering, as a pattern to those who are going to believe on Him for everlasting life (I Timothy 1:16).

KNOWING OUR NEED FOR HIS GRACE STRIKES AT THE MOST DISTASTEFUL ATTITUDE FOUND IN THE HUMAN HEART, OUR PRIDE.

No one will walk in the Spirit at the highest level without an intimate knowledge of the mercy of God. No one deserves His help. Knowing our need for His grace strikes at the most distasteful attitude found in the human heart, our pride. God has only one response to the proud—He resists them. "God resists the proud, but gives grace to the humble" (James 4:6). Jacob and Paul were examples of ones who excelled in spiritual things because they found the mercy of God. We may take hope from the way the Lord poured out kindness upon both of these men.

Jacob Have I Loved, Esau Have I Hated

In view of God's mercy, one might presume that no matter what we do, the Lord will overlook it. However, this presumption greatly affects our relationship with the Lord and restricts His effectiveness in our lives. For this very reason the Lord accepted Jacob and rejected Esau.

> **As it is written, "Jacob I have loved, but Esau I have hated" (Romans 9:13).**

The Amplified Translation provides additional understanding of this difficult verse:

> **As it is written, Jacob have I loved, but Esau have I hated [held in relative disregard in comparison with My feeling for Jacob].**

God's love for Jacob was so great that by comparison His love for Esau was as hatred. Jesus Himself used this idea of comparative love when He said:

> **"If anyone comes to Me and does not hate his father and mother, wife and children, brothers and sisters, yes, and his own life also, he cannot be My disciple" (Luke 14:26).**

Jesus did not encourage us to hate our families, but required us to love Him much more than we love anyone else. Proverbs 8:17 reveals a fundamental characteristic of the Lord. **"I love those who love me, and those who seek me diligently**

will find me." Jacob loved the Lord much more than he did his brother Esau. He so desired the blessing of the Lord that he would stop at nothing to obtain it. As flawed as his methods were, Jacob's relentless pursuit of God captured His heart.

Those God Lightly Esteems

In comparison, Esau so lightly valued eternal things that he sold his God-given birthright for a single meal. We must learn to value what God values and hate what He hates if we are to make progress in the spiritual life. During a dark time in Israel's history, Eli, the high priest and his corrupt sons served in the Tabernacle at Shiloh. Eli's sons took the best of the offerings for themselves and committed sexual immorality with women who were called to serve the Lord. Although Eli rebuked his sons, he did not discipline them or remove them from their priestly office. He also grew fat on the best portions which were designated for the Lord alone. God was not pleased and sent a prophet to Eli who said:

> **"Why then do you kick [trample upon, treat with contempt] My sacrifice and My offering which I commanded, and honor your sons above Me by fattening yourselves upon the choicest part of every offering of My people Israel?**
>
> **Therefore the Lord, the God of Israel, says, I did promise that your house and that of your father [forefather Aaron] should go in and out before Me forever. But now the Lord says, Be it far from Me. For those who honor**

Me I will honor, and those who despise Me shall be lightly esteemed.

Behold, the time is coming when I will cut off your strength and the strength of your own father's house, that there shall not be an old man in your house" (1 Samuel 2:29-31 AMP).

Though mercy is at the core of how the Lord relates to us, our bad attitudes and actions hinder our relationship. Ultimately those who honor the Lord, He will honor, and those who despise Him, He will disdain.

God is Closer Than We First Thought

It is obvious that Jacob grew up convinced that he would only prevail in life by lying and scheming. Had he understood God's heart, he would have lived an entirely different way. When he fled from home that night he had no idea of God's intentions toward him. God set Himself to open Jacob's spiritual eyes.

That night outside of Luz, Jacob was so awestruck and frightened by the encounter he had with the Lord that he gasped. **"Surely the LORD is in this place, and I did not know it"** (Genesis 28:16).

Jacob discovered that God could be found in unexpected places by undeserving people. Even more powerful is the fact that in the New Testament era, God can be found anywhere by anyone who seeks Him by faith. One commentator of the Amplified Bible said of Jacob's discovery: "When Jacob found God in his own heart, he found Him everywhere" (Amplified

Bible, page 36). F.B. Meyer wrote: "There is an open way between heaven and earth for each of us. The movement of the tide and the circulation of the blood are not more regular than the communication between heaven and earth. Jacob may have thought that God was local; now he found Him to be omnipresent. Every lonely spot was His house, filled with angels" (F.B. Meyer, *Through the Bible Day by Day*).

> ULTIMATELY THOSE WHO HONOR THE LORD, HE WILL HONOR, AND THOSE WHO DESPISE HIM, HE WILL DISDAIN.

Every lonely spot is God's house, filled with angels! Jacob made an amazing discovery that evening. His statement: **"How awesome is this place! This is none other than the house of God, and this is the gate of heaven!"** (Genesis 28:17) really meant, "I have found God's house and His door is open to me!" We should be gasping as well every day in light of this glorious reality.

Jacob's experience was but a foreshadowing of the gospel of the kingdom of heaven. Part of Jesus' mission in the earth was to demonstrate, proclaim, and release that kingdom. He told us that the kingdom is at hand, that it is near, and that it is in our midst and yet many are still wondering about it and looking for it. Just as God was with Jacob though he knew it not, so He is with us. Jesus Christ is our "Immanuel," meaning "God with us." It is time for us to stop and realize that wherever we find ourselves, "God is in *this* place even though I did not know it."

Jesus and Nathanael

Jacob's revelation of God began with his dream about a ladder that connected the earth to the heavens. Angels ascended and descended upon it, traversing from the earthly realm into the heavenly one and back again. We gain more insight into the meaning of that ladder from Jesus' meeting with Nathanael:

> **The following day Jesus wanted to go to Galilee, and He found Philip and said to him, "Follow Me."**
>
> **Now Philip was from Bethsaida, the city of Andrew and Peter.**
>
> **Philip found Nathanael and said to him, "We have found Him of whom Moses in the law, and also the prophets, wrote — Jesus of Nazareth, the son of Joseph."**
>
> **And Nathanael said to him, "Can anything good come out of Nazareth?" Philip said to him, "Come and see."**
>
> **Jesus saw Nathanael coming toward Him, and said of him, "Behold, an Israelite indeed, in whom is no deceit!"**
>
> **Nathanael said to Him, "How do You know me?" Jesus answered and said to him, "Before Philip called you, when you were under the fig tree, I saw you."**
>
> **Nathanael answered and said to Him, "Rabbi, You are the Son of God! You are the King of Israel!"**
>
> **Jesus answered and said to him, "Because I said to you, 'I saw you under the fig tree,' do you believe? You will see greater things than these."**
>
> **And He said to him, "Most assuredly, I say to you, hereafter you shall see heaven open, and the angels of God ascending and descending upon the Son of Man" (John 1:43-51).**

JUST AS GOD WAS WITH JACOB THOUGH HE KNEW IT NOT, SO HE IS WITH US.

Jesus knew Nathanael by supernatural revelation and proved it to him when He said, "**Before Philip called you, when** you were under the fig tree, I saw you." In astonishment Nathanael replied, **"Rabbi, You are the Son of God! You are the King of Israel!"** Jesus responded, "Because I said to you, 'I saw you under the fig tree', do you believe? You will see greater things than these...you shall see heaven open, and the angels of God ascending and descending upon the Son of Man."

Heaven Is Open

Jesus identified Himself to Nathanael as the ladder Jacob discovered many years earlier. A ladder is a means of access that rests in two places at the same time, where you are and where you want to be. In Jacob's case that ladder was both in heaven and in the earth simultaneously. In John 3:13 Jesus described Himself to Nicodemus in a similar way, as **"the Son of Man who *is* in heaven."** Meanwhile, He was standing upon the earth as He spoke. Like that ladder, Jesus dwelt in two places at the same time, in the earth and in the heavens. He is the access point between those two realms.

When Jesus told Nathanael that he would see heaven open, He meant that he would see that Jesus is the ladder between the earth and heaven that is wide open to mankind. Jesus did not tell him that he would see heaven *when* it opened, or that he would see heaven on 'opening day' as some momentous event. To Nathanael, He revealed heaven's open disposition toward a dying and needy world. In other words, the kingdom of heaven is at hand.

The Open Door

In Revelation 4 we find a door standing open in heaven:

After these things I looked, and behold, a door standing open in heaven. And the first voice which I heard was like a trumpet speaking with me, saying, "Come up here, and I will show you things which must take place after this."

Immediately I was in the Spirit... (Revelation 4:1-2).

A LADDER IS A MEANS OF ACCESS THAT RESTS IN TWO PLACES AT THE SAME TIME, WHERE YOU ARE AND WHERE YOU WANT TO BE.

The author said, not that he saw the door when it opened, but that it was standing open when he first beheld it. That door is still open today. John then heard this invitation: **"Come up here..."** Interestingly enough, the invitation was to come up. John had a choice to make—to come up or stay where he was. That invitation has not been rescinded and we have the same choice today. When John believed that Jesus had opened a door into the heavens for him, that he had a personal invitation to come up into that place, he was immediately in the Spirit. When we realize that there is a door open in heaven, that we have a personal invitation to come up into that place, our faith can immediately quicken us to experience the very same realm. We are there already, seated together with Christ in heavenly places. We only need to use the access we have been given in Christ.

Our Closed Door

"Behold, I stand at the door and knock. If anyone hears My voice and opens the door, I will come in to him and dine with him, and he with Me" (Revelation 3:20).

Revelation 4 reveals a door that is open in heaven while in Revelation 3 Jesus describes one to the Laodicean church that is closed. The heavenly door is open while the earthly one is closed. He stands there knocking, waiting to come in. Our relationship with Jesus is like two people staying in adjoining motel rooms. Between them stands two doors that separate the rooms. Either party can open his door or keep it closed. Until both are opened, no true communion or communication is shared.

His door is open—what about yours? ■

There is today a pale, pathetic, and unflinching interpretation of the blessed gospel, which guarantees salvation as "a financially and socially upgrading experience;" then it finalizes the offer by "a superlative bonus in eternity and comfort world without end." How different was Paul's concept of a disciple of Christ!

—Leonard Ravenhill

≫≫Mustard Seeds of Wisdom≪≪

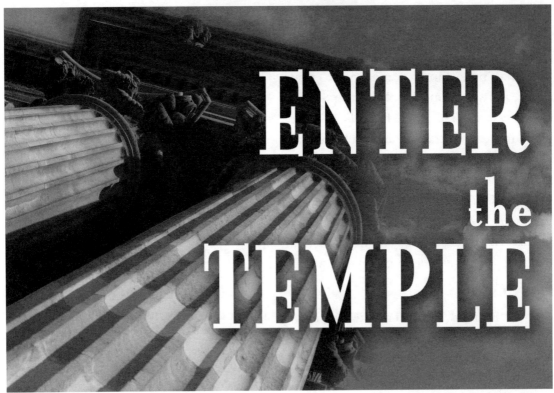

ENTER the TEMPLE

by Steve Thompson

The church in America is entering a season of spectacular expansion unlike anything seen in our generation. Within just a few years, dramatic advances will be coming more quickly than most people now believe possible. To facilitate these advances, a larger segment of the church will become involved in the work of the ministry. However, as the work of the Lord becomes a mandate for many, a temptation will arise that we should recognize and guard against now.

This temptation is very subtle, very dangerous, and very easy to fall into. It is subtle because it plays on our most noble intentions and desires. It is dangerous because it possesses the potential to undermine our greatest calling as leaders. It is easy to fall into because of how we often gauge success in life and ministry.

As the work of the Lord becomes our focus, there will be a temptation to compromise our focus on seeking God, Himself, devotionally. Because of the magnitude of human need, it becomes all too easy for ministering to others to become our number one priority. However, if in an attempt to accomplish more work of ministry, we sacrifice the first work of seeking God, we actually endanger the effectiveness of our ministry.

The Goal of Leadership

Seeking God in a devotional way is the most important ministry we have. Without a vibrant relationship with God, we may touch people superficially, but our impact and influence on their lives will be muted. If we leave off seeking God personally, we may be successful in changing things, but we will ultimately fail to really bring lasting change to people's lives.

Fundamentally, leadership is *inspired influence*. It is the power a leader has to infect people with the desire to change. While some leaders change laws or establish institutions which further their causes, lasting change does not just come from institutions or laws; it comes as people are inspired to seek God and their lives are changed as a result.

OUR GREATEST WORK IS TO HELP PEOPLE CATCH A LOVE FOR AND DESIRE TO KNOW GOD.

It is often said that the greatest lessons are caught more than taught. This is probably more true in spiritual matters than anything else. If those who follow our spiritual leadership are going to "catch something from us," we must possess the thing they need. As leaders in the kingdom of God, our greatest work is to help people catch a love for and desire to know God. This is what

eternal life is about. Consider what Jesus said in John 17:3.

And this is eternal life, that they may know Thee, the only true God, and Jesus Christ whom Thou hast sent (John 17:3).

Ultimately our work of ministry will only last if we provoke people to seek and come to know God. While we are called to do good works and help people practically, our primary calling is to inspire people to seek God. And that will only come as we make meeting with Him our primary calling and work.

We Must Enter

Consider one king of Israel who succeeded in his efforts, but failed in his leadership.

Jotham was twenty-five years old when he became king, and he reigned sixteen years in Jerusalem. And his mother's name was Jerushah the daughter of Zadok.

He did right in the sight of the LORD, according to all that his father Uzziah had done; however he did not enter the temple of the LORD. But the people continued acting corruptly (II Chronicles 27:1-2).

Jotham followed the commandments of God. He was a righteous leader in many respects. He had a successful, functioning kingdom that provided stability for the people. Several verses later we see that Jotham became mighty, because he ordered his ways before the Lord.

But as a leader of the people, Jotham failed because he did not lead the people into righteous living. He did not inspire the people to seek God because as the Scriptures reveal, he failed to **"enter the temple"** himself. When his son became king, he undid many of Jotham's institutional reforms. Since Jotham did not seek God, there was no lasting change brought through his life.

THOSE WHO FOLLOW US WILL ONLY SEEK GOD IF WE SEEK HIM FIRST AND FOREMOST.

It would be tragic for the same to be said of us. We may be successful in our institutional endeavors, but lasting change only comes through inspiring those we lead to love God. All of our efforts at reformation, noble as they may be, will ultimately be ineffective if we do not lead people to God. Those who follow us will only seek God if we seek Him first and foremost. We, unlike Jotham, must keep "going into the temple" our first priority.

The First Works

It requires intentional effort to keep our priorities straight. Historically and biblically, some of the most righteous people have struggled to maintain their priorities. A clear example is the church at Ephesus which Jesus addressed in the Revelation. This was a righteous group of people who were giving their all in serving the Lord. However, their sole failing was maintaining their priority of seeking God first.

Jesus commended the Ephesian church for their works, labor, and commitment to uphold the apostolic standard. They loved righteousness and hated evil. They were fully engaged in their purpose. In fact, the word "Ephesus" means *full purposed*. However, with all of His commendation for them, the Lord had one correction. They had left their first love and their first or primary work.

"I know your deeds and your toil and perseverance, and that you cannot endure evil men, and you put to the test those who call themselves apostles, and they are not, and you found them to be false;

and you have perseverance and have endured for My name's sake, and have not grown weary.

But I have this against you, that you have left your first love.

Remember therefore from where you have fallen, and repent and do the deeds you did

at first; or else I am coming to you, and will remove your lamp stand out of its place—unless you repent" (Revelation 2:2-5).

This passage provides remarkable insight into God's perspective on what makes someone a great leader. In spite of all they were doing correctly, God said that He would remove their lampstand unless they turned around and began doing the first work of seeking Him. Seeking God is the primary calling of leaders.

Your lampstand is your *elevated position of leadership*, established by God, so you can influence and lead others. Our position of leadership was given so we can lead others to God. But if we do not continue to seek God devotionally and draw near to Him, our position of influence will be taken away and given to someone who will. Entering the temple or seeking God is our primary calling.

Working Together Versus Intimacy

More than a decade ago my wife and I worked together for a period of three years. We thought it was a great opportunity because it afforded us so much time together personally, or so we thought. Although we were spending large amounts of time together, much more than the typical couple, it was not really the type of personal time that builds intimate relationships.

When Angie left that job to have our first child, we found that our relationship was actually weaker than before we began working together. We discovered that we had been seduced into believing that we were building our marriage, when we were simply just working together. We had not grown closer by working together; we had just accomplished a lot.

ENTERING THE TEMPLE OR SEEKING GOD IS OUR PRIMARY CALLING.

Additionally, working together can be quite stressful, and this is true of ministry work especially. We discovered that we should have actually increased the amount of time we spent together outside of work in order to build our relationship, but we did the opposite. Thankfully, we recognized this and made a correction fairly quickly after she became a full-time mom.

This is almost a perfect picture of what happens with many church leaders today. As they are engaged in ministry, they experience God's power and presence coming through them and may feel close to Him. However, ministry time is not the same as devotional time and should never be interpreted that way.

Working with the Lord in building His kingdom is an honor and a privilege and it is one way we learn of Him (see Matthew 11:28-30). However, working with God is not a substitute for spending time seeking His face and loving Him. Just as Angie and I discovered that our relationship had weakened because we confused these two things, many leaders have compromised their relationship with the Lord by making the work of the ministry their first priority.

Let's Enter the Garden

God has called us to lead others. Our greatest potential for impact is to lead people to God Himself who transforms them by His Presence. As we fulfill our calling to enter the temple and spend time with God, much more will be accomplished through our lives than we can imagine. But if we fail to stay with our first love and seek Him first, our position of influence, our lampstand, will be removed.

But there is a promise to those who overcome this subtle but powerful temptation to not enter the temple. Consider the promise that Jesus gave to the Ephesian church.

"He who has an ear, let him hear what the Spirit says to the churches. To him who overcomes, I will grant to eat of the tree of life, which is in the Paradise of God" (Revelation 2:7).

Jesus promises us something greater than being able to enter the temple. We will be able to enter the garden of His Presence and partake of the Tree of Life. We can experience eternal life as Jesus described it—knowing the Father and the Son. Let us hear what the Lord is saying to us as leaders and overcome this scheme of the enemy. As we partake of the Tree of Life, we will infect others with a powerful love for God and our leadership will be more effective than ever before. We will lead others to God Himself. ■

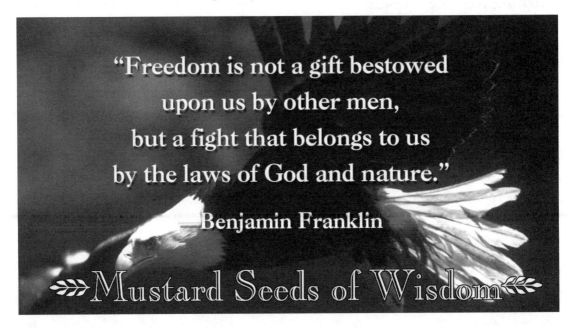

"Freedom is not a gift bestowed
upon us by other men,
but a fight that belongs to us
by the laws of God and nature."

—Benjamin Franklin

≫≫ Mustard Seeds of Wisdom ≪≪

CONSCIENCE: A DIVINE GLOBAL POSITIONING SYSTEM

All Scriptures are New International Version unless otherwise indicated.

by Harry R. Jackson, Jr.

The new generation of prophetic ministry sometimes underestimates the role of the human conscience. While yearning for the spectacular, they often miss the truly supernatural. Remember Balaam, who was famous for the supernatural prophetic gifting in his life? (see Numbers 22-24). Despite his gifting, however, he lost his relationship with God because of an inability to understand the role of his conscience. The English word "conscience" is derived from the word *"conscientia,"* which means three things. First of all, it is the knowledge within; second, it is the moral realm; and third, it is the recognition of distinguishing between good and evil.

All men and women alike have a conscience, but its condition and influence on their words and deeds varies greatly from person to person. For many, their conscience is simply the basis for regret and afterthought. Others are actually prevented from action by the powerful influence of their conscience.

The Silent Gauge

Conscience is like a silent gauge that alerts us to important information. Like a gas or an engine temperature gauge, failure to read this instrument and recognize its messages can be disastrous. We may not get to our destination. In navigating our personal lives we need: (1) the Word of God, (2) the Holy Spirit, (3) circumstances, (4) our conscience.

It is important to realize, a conscience can be developed or damaged. Everyone's inner life is not the same. The New Testament writers talk about a variety of conscience conditions. They speak of those who have a good conscience (see Acts 23:1; I Timothy 1:5,19; Hebrews 13:18; I Peter 3:16,21), a pure conscience (see I Timothy 3:9; II Timothy 1:3), a conscience void of offense (see Acts 24:16), and a conscience that has been purged from the consciousness of sin. They also describe what happens to the consciences of those who have developed the habit of ignoring this inner voice. When a person forges ahead after their own lust or retreats from acknowledging the truth, his or her conscience is weakened.

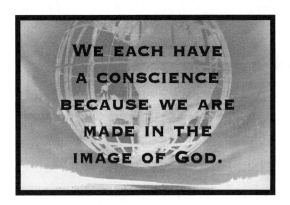

WE EACH HAVE A CONSCIENCE BECAUSE WE ARE MADE IN THE IMAGE OF GOD.

You do not have to be a Christian or even a believer in God to have a conscience. We each have a conscience because we are made in the image of God, which is the rule of God imparted to every man and woman. In fact, those who have never had the opportunity to hear the gospel of Jesus Christ will in the end be judged by how they have responded to their own consciences.

(Indeed, when Gentiles, who do not have the law, do by nature things required by the law, they are a law for themselves, even though they do not have the law,

since they show that the requirements of the law are written on their hearts, their consciences also bearing witness, and their thoughts now accusing, now even defending them.)

This will take place on the day when God will judge men's secrets through Jesus Christ, as my gospel declares (Romans 2:14-16).

According to Paul, judgment will be rendered to unknowing pagans according to what they did with their consciences—whether they acknowledged the moral truth their consciences revealed to them or suppressed that self-evident truth in unrighteousness (see Romans 1:18). They will also be judged by whether they repented because of their consciences' rebuke or forged ahead into sin. Historically, those who rejected the self-evident truth about God were given over to depraved minds and degrading passions, and fell away from God (see Romans 1:24, 26, 28). In the succeeding verses Paul repeats this phrase three times: **"God gave them over"** (to greater degrees of sin). Because they pridefully rejected the convictions of their consciences, the grace of God that restrained them was removed. This is the process through which false religions were birthed after Adam and Eve's fall.

In his letter to Titus, Paul shows that the culture in which we are raised affects our consciences.

Even one of their own prophets has said, "Cretans are always liars, evil brutes, lazy gluttons."

This testimony is true. Therefore, rebuke them sharply, so that they will be sound in the faith

and will pay no attention to Jewish myths or to the commands of those who reject the truth.

To the pure, all things are pure, but to those who are corrupted and do not believe, nothing is pure. In fact, both their minds and consciences are corrupted (Titus 1:12-15).

These are powerful statements, especially when you consider the fact that Paul is referring in this passage to believers. In a fallen culture, people often think they are doing well when they are actually falling far shorter than they realize. Seeing so much sex, violence, and profanity in the media desensitizes our consciences to the extent that we are no longer convicted and appalled by murder, pornography, or a dire lack of integrity.

It is also possible for someone's conscience to malfunction. Titus 1:15 (NKJV) would call this kind of malfunction a "defilement." The word translated "defiled" is the Greek word *miaino*, which means literally "to dye with another color or stain." Those who have not dealt thoroughly with an earlier habit of violating their consciences have a discernable stain on their spirits. Stains of sin can indeed be washed clean by the blood but not without serious repentance and rededication.

We Must Repent

When you make a habit of listening to your conscience, you become more and more sensitive to its voice. Every time you or I ignore the inner moral voice, by whatever rationalization we justify the decision, we defile our consciences. And each time this happens, it becomes a little easier to sin. The inner convictions become a little weaker and the inner voice speaks to us a little softer. Before long, we are able to commit sin without a tinge of conviction. If we continue defiling our consciences each step of the way, we will go into deeper and darker practices. If we do not stop this cycle by repentance, we will eventually end up as reprobates with no discernible conscience at all.

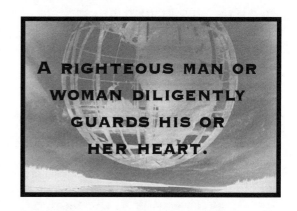

A RIGHTEOUS MAN OR WOMAN DILIGENTLY GUARDS HIS OR HER HEART.

"But solid food is for the mature, who by constant use have trained themselves to distinguish good from evil" (Hebrews 5:14). A righteous man or woman diligently guards his or her heart as a good soldier guards the most strategic of all positions. In time he or she will develop an acute and discerning sensitivity to the inner conscience. We want to readjust our conscience so it is in harmony with the divinely ordained registry, witnessing to right or wrong according to what God thinks and feels.

Our consciences can also come into alignment when we learn to receive correction from trusted spiritual leaders. Just as children must respond to the intense training of loving parents, we must learn that God uses strategic relationships to shape us. These relationships are most typically with local church leaders. Our peers often have the same blind spots that we do; therefore, we must seek out and respond to our chosen mentors and those who disciple us.

As we walk in the power of the love of Christ and the reality of the new birth, our consciences are recalibrated. Repentance may seem like too simple a prescription, but it is very important that we embrace a lifestyle of repentance. Repentance of all known sin is necessary if you and I are going to readjust our consciences. The apostle John wrote:

> **If we claim to have fellowship with him yet walk in the darkness, we lie and do not live by the truth.**
>
> **But if we walk in the light, as he is in the light, we have fellowship with one another, and the blood of Jesus, his Son, purifies us from all sin.**
>
> **If we claim to be without sin, we deceive ourselves and the truth is not in us (I John 1:6-8).**

Covering our sin will produce progressive darkness. Matthew 6:23 says, **"But if your eyes are bad, your whole body will be full of darkness. If then the light within you is darkness, how great is that darkness!"** God sees our twisted nature, which tries to hide from the truth. But when we respond to the convicting power of the Holy Spirit, humble ourselves, and acknowledge the truth, God gives us grace to appropriate all the transforming power of the cross.

COVERING OUR SIN WILL PRODUCE PROGRESSIVE DARKNESS.

Sinners are those who sin by habit and sin by practice. They practice sin and consequently they get better at it. Saints are those who by practice do the right thing, but occasionally sin. Thank God He is going to allow us to receive forgiveness for the sins we do commit and change the areas that are undisciplined and unruly before God.

Spiritual giants are not born ready to impact the world. They are formed and developed by the choices they have made. Make a decision today to live by a code of honor based upon the Word and your conscience. By doing this, you will be an effective member of the body of Christ and a productive participant in the prophetic movement. ∎

THE *Passion* TO CREATE

Scripture reference is New King James Version.

by John Paul Jackson

Whenever I am in Ireland, I am always overwhelmed by the color of the land. The Emerald Isle truly lives up to its name—its greens captivate me, filling every sense. Certainly my eyes testify to the island's beauty, but it is more than that. I can close my eyes and my other senses—including my prophetic feelers, which tell me of the green found in Ireland—the growth, health, vitality, and passion.

The same thing happens when I listen to a great piece of music—my other senses join with my ears to increase my enjoyment of the piece.

Visiting places like Ireland always reaffirm to me God's nature as an Artist. He loves to create and is a diverse Author. The same Being who made the green of Ireland made the pink of Mars and the gold of the Sahara. He made the brightness of the sun and the darkness of the Mariana Trench. Every fiber of His nature loves to create.

When God made man and woman, He placed that same passion in us. Adam and Eve started by creating names for the animals in the Garden of Eden, and they continued by giving birth to and naming their children. Their grandchildren took that creative gift a step further. Genesis 4 records that Cain's sons were the fathers of everyone who built tents, played the harp and flute, and forged tools out of bronze and iron. God's creative power had been imprinted on humanity.

God placed three different entities into every human being: *body*, which includes our flesh, bone, and blood, *soul*, which embodies our mind, will, and emotions, and the *spirit*, which involves the source of wisdom, communion, and conscience. All art—whether writing, painting, making music, singing, turning pots, gardening, sewing, acting, storytelling, filmmaking, or anything else flows from one of the three parts of our being. And the resulting creative output can be classified in three ways, according to the entity of our being from which they spring forth: productive art, creative art, and spiritual art.

THE HUMAN SPIRIT IS WHAT CONNECTS US TO GOD.

1) **Productive art** is sparked when the artist's *body* is in control. This type of art is focused on doing, accomplishing goals, and reaching a mandated quantity or volume. For writers, it is manifested in a number of words that must be churned out. Left unchecked, it will turn our artistic expression into a job because the battle against time will consume us. Productive art does not change anyone or anything for a significant amount of time.

2) **Creative art** is produced by the *soul* and can also be called imaginative art. Our human emotions generate a passion to create art, while our will desires to capture those feelings. Our mind then fuses this soulish passion and desire, producing a complete effort. Soulish artists feel as though they have to think something up and formulate ideas. Creative art can change a person for the short-term, but it has no long-term effect on its viewers.

3) **Spiritual art** flows from our *spirit's* communion with the Holy Spirit. It communicates from the creator's spirit to the viewer's spirit through the power of the Holy Spirit. The human spirit is what connects us to God. There is an intermingling between the two through the process of redemption, resulting in a transformation of the spirit. The spirit then uses the soul and body to produce incredible work.

I believe that only a person who is filled with the Holy Spirit can develop spiritual art that is transformational. The world acts from the soul, and there are times when you can picture the author's meaning. However, I am convinced that only a spiritual artist, writer, or musician can transcend that realm because when the Spirit communicates, it is transformational. The Spirit's work can result in an eternal change in a reader's life.

People visit the Sistine Chapel and are changed forever by what they see of the magnificence of God. The same thing happens when one visits Ireland's many grand abbeys. Books are produced every year, some of which transform the soul of those who digest their pages. "I will not be the same; I have been altered by this insight" the reader says. While soulish or creative art can cause temporary change in a person, spiritual art will change a person for eternity.

The challenge for us, therefore, is to listen carefully to the heartbeat of the Holy Spirit. We must clean out the issues that keep our soul in the driver's seat of our lives; we need to yield ourselves to the rule of the Holy Spirit. It takes discipline and practice to fully understand the distinction between what is our own soul and what God is speaking to us in the Spirit. We must be committed to allowing His essence to flow through us.

I believe that God wants us to create today what will inspire people tomorrow. He has a vantage point of eternity that shows what will be, not what is. Sadly, many of us have been content to grasp at slivers of revelation, but the Holy Spirit wants to give us fuller concepts. He wants to enrich and infuse our creative endeavors with more of His light.

My favorite Bible verse shares a hint of the kind of outlandish, outrageous creativity God wants us to flow in: **"Eye has not seen, nor ear heard, nor have entered into the heart of man the things which God has prepared for those who love Him" (I Corinthians 2:9).**

> I BELIEVE THAT GOD WANTS US TO CREATE TODAY WHAT WILL INSPIRE PEOPLE TOMORROW.

In your chosen creative endeavors, try to capture the deep mysteries of God. Too often we have settled for creating from our soul or body when a higher call has been trying to reach us.

Remember, what you develop will determine the people you reach and how your work affects them. May we learn to create from our spirit, seeing spiritual fruit that comes from our endeavors: love, joy, peace, longsuffering, kindness, goodness, faithfulness, gentleness, and self-control. The world is waiting! ■

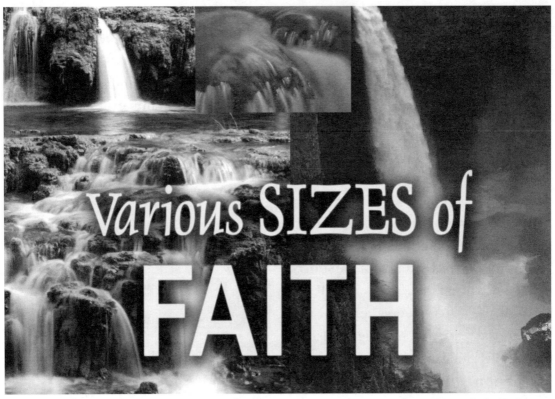

Various SIZES of FAITH

All Scriptures are New International Version.

by Randal Cutter

everal years ago I had a conversation with a *Coca Cola* executive about the variety of sizes in which his company bottles its product. Our discussion included such terms as market forces and price points. He mentioned that people love choices.

Christians have several sizes of faith from which to choose. Faith does not come in as many sizes as soft drinks, but it does come in at least three distinct sizes. Jesus demonstrated this when He chided those with little faith, praised those with great faith, and encouraged His followers to walk in faith.

What size faith do you choose? We will examine the different sizes of faith so that we can choose the correct size for our lives.

Little Faith

Jesus revealed a great deal about faith when He chided those who had little of it. On six different occasions Jesus told people they had little faith. In every instance He was speaking to people in covenant with God. These people had history with God, yet still had little faith. When we look more closely at several of these instances, we learn just what constitutes little faith.

In the Sermon on the Mount, Jesus addressed how inappropriate it was for God's people to worry about food or clothing. After pointing to the beauty of the flowers around them, Jesus asked, **"If that is how God clothes the grass of the field, which is here today and tomorrow is thrown into the fire, will** he not much more clothe you, O you of little faith?" (Matthew 6:30) His point is clear. Every one of the people around Jesus had observed God's care of birds and flowers. Their experience taught them that God takes good care of such relatively minor things. Thus, it was not rational to conclude that He would treat His chosen people with less care. When the people of Jesus' day worried about food and clothing, they did not live up to their experience of God's care. Jesus summed it up by saying they had little faith.

When Jesus calmed the storm we see these same themes. A severe storm on the sea of Galilee tested the mettle of Jesus' disciples. As the storm began to overwhelm them, the disciples cried out to the sleeping Jesus. As Jesus woke up He said to them, "You of little faith, why are you so afraid?" (Matthew 8:26) Then, with a word, He calmed the storm.

From a non-faith perspective, it is quite apparent why the disciples were afraid. Huge waves were swamping their boat, and these experienced fishermen understood the gravity of the situation. Over the years, they had seen friends and neighbors in their fishing community disappear in tempests such as this one. They were convinced they were all about to drown. From a purely natural perspective, they were behaving rationally. But the disciples had been living the supernatural with Jesus for quite some time. They had history with Jesus and lots of it. Yet they allowed their previous life experiences to trump that supernatural experience. Because they had experienced His great love and power, it was irrational for them to believe that He would allow them to drown. They were not living up to their experience with Jesus.

This problem plagued the disciples. The most obvious example of this is recorded in Matthew 16. Jesus had just finished feeding five thousand men, in addition to the women and children, with five loaves of bread and a few fish. He had followed up that miracle with the feeding of the four thousand under similar conditions. Yet when the disciples forgot to bring bread for a journey, they concluded that this would leave them bereft of lunch. Jesus quite explicitly led them down the road of logic to show them the type of faith they were demonstrating.

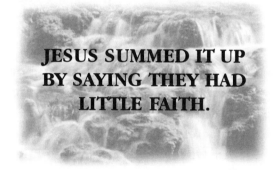

JESUS SUMMED IT UP BY SAYING THEY HAD LITTLE FAITH.

...Jesus asked, "You of little faith, why are you talking among yourselves about having no bread?

Do you still not understand? Don't you remember the five loaves for the five thousand, and how many basketfuls you gathered?

Or the seven loaves for the four thousand, and how many basketfuls you gathered?" (Matthew 16:8-10)

Jesus had fed tens of thousands of people with less than a grocery bag of food. It is only logical to conclude that in a pinch He could handle lunch for a dozen. More than that, their experience of His generous care of all these people made it impossible to assume that He would callously ignore the plight of His closest disciples. The littleness of their faith was staggering. But often, so is ours.

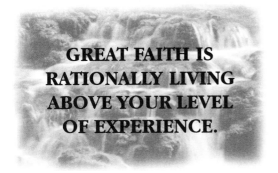

GREAT FAITH IS RATIONALLY LIVING ABOVE YOUR LEVEL OF EXPERIENCE.

Jesus once said, **"…when the Son of Man comes, will he find faith on the earth?" (Luke 18:8)** While faith may be scarce when He returns, I do not believe He will have any problem finding little faith. We can easily find that all around us. It occurs whenever we, like Jesus' disciples, do not live up to our experience of God's love and His power. I have seen many examples of God's love and power demonstrated through miraculous healings. I have seen my own family touched in amazing ways, and I have felt His healing hand personally. Yet there are times when I am assaulted with concerns about my own or my family's health that I am tempted to worry. Since I have experienced God's love and His power in this area, if I do step into worry, I am demonstrating little faith. It is rational to believe that God is faithful and consistent in these areas. He is the same yesterday, today, and forever (see Hebrews 13:8). We can build our faith for the future upon our experiences of His love and power in the past. If we do not do this, we are demonstrating little faith.

This applies to every area of life. If the Lord has provided a miraculous financial deliverance for us, we can rationally expect that He will be faithful in this area again. If the Lord has provided physical healing, we can rationally expect the Healer to be faithful in this area again. When we experience the Lord's faithfulness in an area, it is only faith to expect that the Lord will repeat that kindness.

This truth is exactly the reason that Jesus told Peter he had little faith right after he walked on water. From our perspective, Peter demonstrated incredible faith when he stepped out of the boat onto a stormy sea. Yet, when Jesus stooped down to pull the sinking Peter back to the surface of the waves, He said to him, **"You of little faith" (Matthew 14:31).** There is little doubt that when Peter stepped out of the boat he was demonstrating faith, perhaps even great faith. His quick demotion to little faith was found in his irrational doubt. In the midst of miraculously breaking several laws of physics, he began to believe those laws were more powerful than this miracle. He did not live up to the level of his miraculous experience, even while he was experiencing it.

Great Faith

If little faith is irrationally living below your experience of God, then, conversely, great faith is rationally living above your level of experience. Jesus clearly demonstrated this when He praised two Gentiles who walked in great faith.

It is not coincidence that Jesus only applied the great faith label to Gentiles. The Gentiles of Jesus' day had little experience of the true God. The Roman centurion (see Matthew 8:5) and the Canaanite woman (see Matthew 15:21) grew up in nations with demonic understandings of deity. Their national gods were demanding, capricious, and vicious. These pagan cultures bribed and placated their gods, rather than loving or trusting them. They understood little of God's goodness and grace. Yet both of these individuals stepped beyond their experience. They also gave solid reasons for their steps of faith.

The centurion's servant was sick when he encountered Jesus. Jesus acted according to Jewish custom and agreed to go to the servant's side. In Jewish culture, it was normal for those who prayed for healing to make a personal appearance (see Matthew 9:18). Jesus usually followed this custom in order to remove unnecessary barriers to faith.

When the centurion, who had not grown up under the Covenant, sought Jesus' help, he was demonstrating faith. Jesus responded to this faith in His normal fashion. However, the centurion soon demonstrated greatness in his faith.

> **The centurion replied, "Lord, I do not deserve to have you come under my roof. But just say the word, and my servant will be healed" (Matthew 8:8).**

With these words, the centurion displayed great faith. With his first request, the centurion demonstrated that he had moved beyond his own cultural experience and now believed in the goodness of God. With his second request, he demonstrated that he had moved beyond even the Jewish cultural understanding of how God worked. Whereas Jewish theology expected some form of contact to initiate a miracle, this centurion believed a word spoken at a distance would be equally powerful.

> **IT IS NOT COINCIDENCE THAT JESUS ONLY APPLIED THE GREAT FAITH LABEL TO GENTILES.**

To those who traveled with Jesus, this may have seemed like presumption. How dare this centurion presume to tell Jesus how to operate His ministry? But this was not presumption. Presumption is irrational in its character. Presumption moves beyond our experience of God in irrational ways. The centurion did not do this. Instead, he offered a rational explanation for his belief.

> **For I myself am a man under authority, with soldiers under me. I tell this one, "Go," and he goes; and that one, "Come," and he comes. I say to my servant, "Do this," and he does it (Matthew 8:9).**

The centurion recognized the nature of authority. If the centurion, with only a word, could affect outcomes at a distance, then Jesus should be able to do the same thing. The centurion stepped ahead of his experience of God as he applied his understanding of authority to God's kingdom in a logical way.

The Canaanite woman demonstrated this same type of logical insight. When Jesus had insulted her by comparing her to a dog, she said, "**…but even the dogs eat the crumbs that fall from their masters' table" (Matthew 15:27).** Jesus purposely baited her and she refused to choke on the bait. Instead she first demonstrated faith. She recognized that it would only take supernatural crumbs for an almighty God to heal her daughter. Then she demonstrated great faith. She inferred some things about God's kingdom based upon Jesus' own Words. If a dog's master allows him to eat the crumbs that fall below the table, how much more would a righteous and merciful God provide the crumbs of His supernatural grace to people in need. Rather than turning away insulted and sad, she lived beyond her experience of God and received her answer.

In essence, great faith stands on the foundation of our experience with God, builds a reasonable case for things we have not yet experienced, and takes action based upon that belief. However, while Jesus applauded great faith and was pleased by it, He does not demand great faith from us.

Faith

The apostle John penned words which speak with our experience of God: **"We love because he first loved us" (I John 4:19).** Faith responds to the grace which

God has given. It experiences something of God and then responds to it. We became Christians through this process. We experienced the promise of God's forgiveness, and we lived up to this experience by making a life commitment to Him. This is faith.

God continues to demonstrate His goodness in many ways. When we respond to that goodness, and act according to it, we are living by faith. When our actions do not live up to the goodness which we have experienced, that is little faith. When we have not yet experienced God's goodness in a particular area of our life, but we are able to build a rational case for believing God, then this is great faith.

Conclusion

The writer to the Hebrews tells us, **"…without faith it is impossible to please God…" (Hebrews 11:6).** This is more than an axiom to inspire a more committed life of faith; it is the foundation of our Christian walk. Christians live by faith from start to finish (see Romans 1:17). For this reason Jude wrote, **"But you, dear friends, build yourselves up in your most holy faith…" (Jude 1:20).** I believe when we better understand the process of faith, we can better build our faith. It is apparent that greatness or smallness of faith is not found in the size of the supernatural events in which we are involved, but rather in how well we are living up to our experience with God and His faithfulness. When we focus on His grace in our lives, and determine to live up to that grace, we build up our most holy faith. ■

Neglecting Our AUTHORITY

by John Hansen

Of all people, Eliashib should have known better. As high priest for the entire nation of Israel, he was responsible for the temple administration and the food distribution for the city's ministry team. He was Israel's senior pastor and worship leader, and was responsible for ensuring that the people of God were living holy. If he were to be slack in his duties, not only would his fellow ministers suffer, but so would the entire nation. With all this responsibility, one would think he would take his job seriously. But apparently he was not serious enough. The principle he failed to learn was, if someone does not use their authority when they should, then they are guilty of abusing it.

The account of Eliashib's dereliction of duty (see Nehemiah 13) exemplifies for us the principle that neglect leads to loss (see Proverbs 24:30-34). What makes the account of Eliashib even more sobering is that his downfall was self-inflicted and avoidable. Therefore, it is vital that we learn from his mistakes so we do not fall into this vicious circle of passivity and compromise.

Eliashib's Negligence

Eliashib came from a rich spiritual heritage. Born into the line of Aaron and Zadok, he inherited the awesome mantle of high priest. His grandfather, in fact, was the famed Joshua, the first high priest after the Babylonian captivity in 536 B.C. (see Nehemiah 12:10-11). The prophet Zechariah even prophesied that Joshua would be a type of the coming Messiah (see Zechariah 3 and 6). Eliashib was following in the footsteps of those select few who had the rare privilege of ministering before God in the Holy of Holies. Moreover, the very meaning of Eliashib's name—"Jehovah has restored"—prophetically epitomized the times in which he lived, the Restoration Period from 538 B.C. to 430 B.C. Surely he was destined for greatness.

When Eliashib first appeared in the biblical record, we see him exercising his priestly authority by rallying his fellow priests to rebuild Jerusalem (see Nehemiah 3:1). Initially, he zealously supported Nehemiah and Ezra's reforms. But somewhere along the way he lost sight of the seriousness of his calling. And when that happened, carelessness and compromise were inevitable.

SOMEWHERE ALONG THE WAY HE LOST SIGHT OF THE SERIOUSNESS OF HIS CALLING.

Eliashib's downfall occurred when he did the unthinkable: He **"prepared a large room"** in the temple for God's enemy, Tobiah the Ammonite, to occupy! (see Nehemiah 13:5) Ironically, Tobiah's name means "Jehovah is good." Tobiah, you may recall, tormented the Jews during their rebuilding of Jerusalem, saying that their walls would collapse if a mere fox jumped on them (see Nehemiah 4:3). In short, Tobiah made it his business to mock and frustrate the purposes of God (see Nehemiah 4:7-8; 6:12-14).

So why would a high priest do something so blatantly wrong by aiding and abetting the enemy? Possibly it was because Tobiah was Eliashib's relative (see Nehemiah 13:4). That is no excuse, however, because it was Eliashib's job as God's representative to uphold the law that the Jews disassociate themselves from all Ammonites like Tobiah (see Deuteronomy 23:3). Instead, he let this **"accuser of the brethren"**(Revelation 12:10 KJV) live under the same roof as the Holy of Holies.

But Eliashib's compromise did not happen overnight. Rather, it was the natural consequence of his being casual or careless with what God entrusted to him. His compromise first began when he failed to heed Solomon's advice to guard his heart (see Proverbs 4:23). As a result of his courting the enemies of his soul—namely fear of man, selfish ambition, and lust for comfort—it became easy for him to surrender to the enemy of his people.

The room Eliashib turned over to Tobiah was a storeroom for the tithes, offerings, oil, and wine that were to be distributed to the Levites, singers, and temple gatekeepers (see Nehemiah 13:5). Evidently, while Eliashib was busy entertaining Tobiah, he neglected to give the temple staff their due reward, which prompted them to quit and go **"each to his own field"** to fend for themselves (see Nehemiah 13:10). This is another sad case of how one leader's irresponsibility affected so many others. Because Eliashib made **"provision for the flesh" (Romans 13:14)** by willfully granting room to the enemy, Satan took advantage of him and his countrymen.

Rectifying the Damage

When Governor Nehemiah returned to Jerusalem and discovered **"the evil"** (Nehemiah 13:7) that Eliashib had done, he attempted to rectify the damage. First, he lamented over how this one indolent priest destroyed all the good he worked so hard to accomplish. But then Nehemiah did what Eliashib never did—he exercised his authority by throwing **"all of Tobiah's household goods out of the room" (Nehemiah 13:8)**. After that, the governor ordered the rooms cleansed and restored to their proper use for holding the ministry utensils, grain offerings, and frankincense.

Next, Nehemiah reprimanded the leaders for their negligence and reinstated the backslidden ministry staff. Before long, **"all Judah then brought the tithe of the grain, wine, and oil into the storehouses" (Nehemiah 13:12).** He also reinstituted the Sabbath-keeping laws and the ban on interfaith marriages. As a final act, Nehemiah expelled Eliashib's delinquent grandson, who married a daughter of Tobiah's notorious cohort, Sanballat the Horonite (see Nehemiah 13:28).

It is a sad commentary that the last record of Eliashib's life was about his moral failure that created widespread devastation. Nehemiah, in fact, inferred in the closing of his book that Eliashib's family **"defiled the priesthood and the covenant of the priesthood and the Levites" (Nehemiah 13:29).** Because this once zealous leader became passive with his authority, he jeopardized not only his own calling, but also the spiritual welfare of the entire nation.

The Application

The main lesson of Eliashib's downfall is this: If we are not using our God-given authority when necessary, then we are abusing it. Like Eliashib, how many times have we given room in our lives for the enemy to set up shop? I believe Eliashib found it difficult to exercise his authority simply because he compromised beforehand with the "enemies" of his soul. These "soul-enemies" often come in the form of a fear of man, selfish ambition, lust for

comfort, or self-pity. But thankfully, the Lord has given us the authority through His Spirit to mortify these deeds of the flesh, if we would but use that authority.

HOW MANY TIMES HAVE WE GIVEN ROOM IN OUR LIVES FOR THE ENEMY TO SET UP SHOP?

Besides our being responsible for ourselves, we all carry authority outside of ourselves to some degree, whether it is with our families, friends, jobs, or communities. Imagine what can happen when we become passive with the responsibilities and spiritual authority Christ has delegated to us. How many children are going astray because their parents are neglecting to use their authority? How many are facing needless battles because their spouses neglect to seriously pray for them? How many church, business, and school issues are escalating into crises because people are passive with their authority?

The point is God gives us authority because He expects us to use it. Just like in the parable of the talents, if we bury a responsibility that He has delegated to us, we jeopardize losing it—and much more (see Matthew 25:24-30). Therefore, let us ask the Lord to expose any "Eliashib" areas that we have neglected and grant to us Nehemiah's focus and initiative to rectify them. If we become passive with our authority like Eliashib, who knows what price we might have to pay. ■

Staying On The PATH OF LIFE

by Rick Joyner

"**Enter by the narrow gate; for the gate is wide, and the way is broad that leads to destruction, and many are those who enter by it.**

"**For the gate is small, and the way is narrow that leads to life, and few are those who find it**" (Matthew 7:13-14).

When a path is narrow, you will be much more careful how you walk. Likewise, when a path is broad, you do not have to be as careful. In the exhortation above, the Lord is warning us to be very careful how we walk because the path that leads to life is very narrow. This is by design. To be careful means to be "full of care." To be careless means to "care less." Those who do not care enough about life to be full of care in how they walk will sooner or later stumble, and depart from it.

My brother recently remarked to me how he thought it was strange that so many Christian leaders seem to fall into sin near the end of their lives. This has been far too common. It seems the longer we walk with the Lord and the more we have been used by Him, the more careless we might become in our walk. Could it be that this causes a subtle form of pride to arise in our hearts? As we are told in Proverbs 16:18-19:

Pride goes before destruction, and a haughty spirit before stumbling.

It is better to be of a humble spirit with the lowly, than to divide the spoil with the proud.

The humble are inherently more careful. The proud will inherently become more careless, which in due time will inevitably lead to a fall. So how can we guard ourselves from this?

First, the Christian walk is called a "walk" because we are going somewhere. The path indicates a way that leads to a destination. If we are not growing and progressing, at the very least we will stagnate, which is a tragic spiritual condition.

We must also realize that as we mature in the Lord the path we walk upon does not get broader, but even narrower. With greater light comes greater responsibility. It is true that the things the priests could get away with in the Outer Court would get them killed in the Holy Place. The greater our anointing in ministry, the less we can get away with—not more.

One of the most basic characteristics of humility is to be teachable and correctable. Those who are humble are ever seeking to grow in knowledge, wisdom, and understanding. Some of the best instruction we will ever receive will come from learning the reasons for our mistakes. That is why Proverbs 10:17 states:

He is on the path of life who heeds instruction, but he who forsakes reproof goes astray.

The book of Proverbs establishes one thing very clearly—the wise love reproof and fools reject it. Consider this statement from Proverbs 3:11-12:

My son, do not reject the discipline of the Lord, or loathe His reproof,

for whom the Lord loves He reproves, even as a father, the son in whom he delights.

AS WE MATURE IN THE LORD THE PATH WE WALK UPON DOES NOT GET BROADER, BUT EVEN NARROWER.

By this we must understand that correction and reproof should not be taken as rejection, but as evidence of God's love for us. In fact, the scariest thing in the world should be if we are transgressing and getting away with it. If we are His children, He will correct us because He loves us. As Hebrews 12:8 states, **"But if you are without discipline, of which all have become partakers, then you are illegitimate children and not sons."** Think about that. If we are not being disciplined, it is evidence that we are not His children. For this reason we should greatly esteem correction and discipline as the great treasure that it is.

It was said of King Solomon that he chaffed under his father's discipline and complained that he received far more reproof and correction than his brothers. This is because Solomon had a higher calling—his brothers were not called to be the king. If we are receiving greater discipline and correction, it is likely because of our calling. Likewise, the things that come too easily or quickly are usually insignificant. This includes our callings and ministries.

IF WE ARE RECEIVING GREATER DISCIPLINE AND CORRECTION, IT IS LIKELY BECAUSE OF OUR CALLING.

Carefully consider what wisdom personified states in Proverbs 1:23, 25-33:

Turn to my reproof, behold, I will pour out my spirit on you; I will make my words known to you.

And you neglected all my counsel, and did not want my reproof,

I will even laugh at your calamity; I will mock when your dread comes,

when your dread comes like a storm, and your calamity comes on like a whirlwind, when distress and anguish come on you.

Then they will call on me, but I will not answer; they will seek me diligently, but they shall not find me,

because they hated knowledge, and did not choose the fear of the Lord.

They would not accept my counsel, they spurned all my reproof.

So they shall eat of the fruit of their own way, and be satiated with their own devices.

For the waywardness of the naive shall kill them, and the complacency of fools shall destroy them.

But he who listens to me shall live securely, and shall be at ease from the dread of evil.

We may think this is too severe, but we must realize we are playing for the highest stakes of all—eternal life itself! A soldier in training may hate his drill sergeant, but when he gets into battle he will love him and be thankful for his severity. We will be the same concerning the Lord's severe discipline in our life. This is no game. Those who take it lightly are the ones who care-less, and will therefore be careless with their walk.

Further consider these exhortations from the book of wisdom, Proverbs:

Whoever loves discipline loves knowledge, but he who hates reproof is stupid (12:1).

Poverty and shame will come to him who neglects discipline, but he who regards reproof will be honored (13:18).

A fool rejects his father's discipline, but he who regards reproof is prudent (15:5).

Stern discipline is for him who forsakes the way; he who hates reproof will die (15:10).

He whose ear listens to the life-giving reproof will dwell among the wise (15:31).

He who neglects discipline despises himself, but he who listens to reproof acquires understanding.

The fear of the Lord is the instruction for wisdom, and before honor comes humility (15:32-33).

A man who hardens his neck after much reproof will suddenly be broken beyond remedy (29:1).

The rod and reproof give wisdom, but a child who gets his own way brings shame to his mother (29:15).

Of course, when the Lord disciplines us a big hand does not reach out of heaven and spank us. There are a number of ways the Lord disciplines His people, ranging from speaking through a donkey, to having His angel confront us. He does not tend to use the method that we like the most, but the one we need the most.

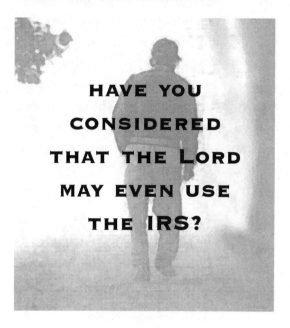

HAVE YOU CONSIDERED THAT THE LORD MAY EVEN USE THE IRS?

One of His methods of correction, which is probably the most irritating and therefore requires the most humility to receive, is by using the heathen or even our enemies. This is why the Lord continually used the heathen nations around Israel to discipline His people for their apostasies. Have you considered that the Lord is actually using your boss? He may even be trying to use your neighbors who seem so unreasonable. It could even be the Lord provoking that traffic cop who seems especially intent on giving you tickets. Or, God forbid, have you considered that the Lord may even use the IRS?

It is also noteworthy that after the Lord used the heathen nations, He would then judge them for attacking Israel because of their "arrogance" in touching the Lord's people! That does not seem fair does it? However, the Lord did not give those heathen nations their arrogance—He just used it for the sake of His people. That is why we should not reject correction that comes from our enemies. Our enemies will tell us things our friends will not, but things that we need to hear. Of course, this does not mean we should accept everything our enemies say about us, but we should be sensitive to any truth in it that we need to hear.

A TRUE FRIEND WILL TELL US THE TRUTH WHEN WE ARE MAKING A MISTAKE.

Another source of correction should be our friends. As Proverbs 27:6 states, the wounds of a friend are more desirable than the kisses of an enemy. A friend, who is a true friend, will tell us the truth when we are making a mistake. A true friend will even risk our rejection to tell us what we need to hear because they are thinking more of us than their acceptance.

I have had so called friends, and even ministry team members, tell me after a mistake or problem that they knew prophetically beforehand something was going to happen, as if this would actually encourage me. Because they had this knowledge and did not tell me beforehand when it could have helped, it therefore greatly reduced the trust I had in them as a friend. If we have knowledge that someone is going to make a mistake or have problems, and do not warn them, how will we ever be true shepherds or watchmen?

On the other hand, I have also learned not to give much credence to someone who tends to only have warnings. If we follow the paranoid, we will make far more mistakes than we will if we are moving forward in faith. There are also some things we are called to do that will cause problems, but they are problems which are inevitable. Although it is good to know beforehand that the problems will come, it does not mean we should change our course, but rather just be prepared.

For example, the Lord could not have fulfilled His own purpose on the earth if He was overly concerned about the problems that His teachings would cause the religious elite of the times. If we walk and serve in His Spirit, we will stir up the same opposition He did. It will also come from the religious, ultra conservatives who consider themselves to be the true protectors of the faith, but have actually been self-appointed.

Now my philosophy is "no pain, no pain." By this I mean that I am not into pain and will try to avoid it if possible. I would rather have the pain of discipline if I need it, but I would rather not need it. A great promise for this is I Corinthians 11:31: **"But if we judged ourselves rightly, we should not be judged."** This could have been translated as "If we discerned ourselves correctly we would not have to be disciplined." Or, if we would discipline ourselves, the Lord would not have to do it. That is by far the easier way. If we would fall on the Rock and be broken, He would not have to fall on us and crush us into powder.

However, who can be so unbiased about themselves to be able to discern their own hearts, motives, and actions? Read what the apostle Paul said about this in I Corinthians 4:1-5:

> **Let a man regard us in this manner, as servants of Christ, and stewards of the mysteries of God.**
>
> **In this case, moreover, it is required of stewards that one be found trustworthy.**
>
> **But to me it is a very small thing that I should be examined by you, or by any human court; in fact, I do not even examine myself.**
>
> **I am conscious of nothing against myself, yet I am not by this acquitted; but the one who examines me is the Lord.**
>
> **Therefore do not go on passing judgment before the time, but wait until the Lord comes who will both bring to light the things hidden in the darkness and disclose the motives of men's hearts; and then each man's praise will come to him from God.**

IF WE WOULD DISCIPLINE OURSELVES, THE LORD WOULD NOT HAVE TO DO IT.

Paul was saying here that he did not even examine himself, but waited for the Lord to examine him. Now Paul obviously did not mean this in all things, as he later wrote in the same letter for the people to examine themselves before taking communion (see I Corinthians 11:28). In his next letter to the same people he exhorted them to examine themselves to be sure that they remained in the faith (see II Corinthians 13:5). This is not a contradiction as the immature might interpret it, but rather a distinction. There are things in which we can examine ourselves, and there are matters where we really cannot be impartial and should wait for the Lord's judgment in the matter. It is wisdom to know the difference, and I believe it would be in any matter where we honestly know that we are not clear.

One of the primary ways that the Lord examines us is through His written Word, the Scriptures. As Paul wrote in II Timothy 3:16-17:

All Scripture is inspired by God and profitable for teaching, for reproof, for correction, for training in righteousness;

that the man of God may be adequate, equipped for every good work.

Those who have Bibles and do not read them daily are not only neglecting one of the greatest treasures we have been given on this earth, but they are causing themselves many unnecessary problems in this life because the Lord has to discipline them in areas they could have corrected themselves.

Spurgeon lamented that he could find ten men who would die for the Bible for every one who would read it! Anyone who has the attitude that they have to read the Bible every day should consider themselves to have either backslidden or are still very immature. It is not that we *have* to read the Bible, but that we *get* to! It will teach us, reprove us when we need it, correct us, and train us so that we are adequate for every work we have been called to.

We should desire the Scriptures more than we do food or drink. They are life to us. Those who truly love the Word Himself will also love His Word, and they will love the correction that it gives them,

knowing it is sparing them from having to receive it in a much more difficult way.

So, consider that the correction which comes to us from the Lord is evidence of His love for us, not His rejection. The more severe it is, the higher the calling. Do not remorse that you cannot get away with what others may seem to be getting away with—embrace your love from the Lord!

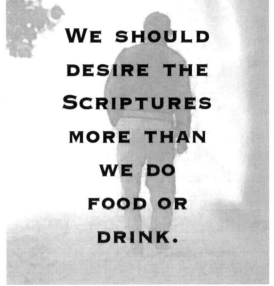

WE SHOULD DESIRE THE SCRIPTURES MORE THAN WE DO FOOD OR DRINK.

Also, always keep in mind Proverbs 4:18, which states: **"But the path of the righteous is like the light of dawn, that shines brighter and brighter until the full day."** If we are on the path of the righteous, the path of life, then we should be walking in ever increasing light. If this is not true for us, then somewhere we have departed from the path. As C.S. Lewis observed, in the Lord the wrong path never turns into the right path, but if we would get on the right path we must go back to where we missed the turn. This is called repentance. The ability to quickly and profoundly repent is one of the most sure signs of true spiritual maturity. ∎

The SONG of the LAMB

by Lilo Keller

The song of the Lamb and the roaring of the Lion are very powerful images depicting two different aspects of the character of God. Although very different, they are inseparable. In fact, they complement each other, allowing us to look into the inexpressible depth, width, height, and length of the love of God. I am convinced that God, represented by "the Lion of Judah," has risen up to fight for us, His bride, in order for us to hear and learn from Him the "song of the Lamb."

The Lamb as the Sacrifice

The Lamb as the sacrifice for the redemption of God's people is mentioned in the beginning of the Bible in Exodus, as well as in the end in Revelation.

The night when the angel of death passed through Egypt slaying every first born, the blood of the Lamb was the shield of protection for the people of Israel. They kept the living animals in their houses for three days, killed them on the prescribed evening, spread the blood on their doorposts, and then ate the meat. By doing this they remained untouched by the angel of death. The next morning they were finally delivered from their slavery under the Egyptian Pharaoh. Through the redemption of His people, God prophetically foreshadowed His final plan of redemption and restoration.

In his song about the servant of the Lord, Isaiah once again gives us a picture of the Lamb being led to the slaughter (see Isaiah 53). He prophetically announced the sacrifice of Jesus Christ who would atone for all sin, infirmity, and shame through His sacrifice, thus establishing an access to His heavenly Father for all peoples, tribes, and nations.

After His resurrection, Jesus entrusted His disciple, John, with the revelation of how His obedience, willingness to die on the cross, resurrection, and ascension to heaven would impact the history of mankind.

The Turning Point in Heaven

In a vision, John saw the Father sitting on the throne. In His right hand He was holding a scroll inscribed on both sides and sealed with seven seals.

But no one in heaven or on earth or under the earth could open the scroll or even look inside it.

I (John) wept and wept because no one was found who was worthy to open the scroll or look inside.

Then one of the elders said to me, "Do not weep! See, the Lion of the tribe of Judah, the Root of David, has triumphed. He is able to open the scroll and its seven seals" (Revelation 5:3-5).

Jesus, the mighty One of the tribe of Judah (see Genesis 49:9-10) is able to open the scroll.

The focus suddenly shifted. It was not the Lion representing the strong, assertive, and majestic side of God who is granted permission to receive the book, but it was the Lamb, a symbol of meekness, humility, and total self-dedication. The Lamb was crucified and is alive. For the first time, John saw and described the exalted Lamb of God.

"Then I saw a Lamb, looking as if it had been slain, standing in the center of the throne, **encircled by the four living creatures and the elders. He had seven horns and seven eyes, which are the seven spirits of God sent out into all the earth.**

He came and took the scroll from the right hand of him who sat on the throne (Revelation 5:6-7).

As a sign of His ultimate power and authority, the Lamb has seven horns (seven being the number of perfection and holiness). He has seven eyes, symbolizing the knowledge and wisdom given to Him through the Holy Spirit as described in Isaiah 11:2: **"The Spirit of the LORD will rest on him—the Spirit of wisdom and of understanding, the Spirit of counsel and of power, the Spirit of knowledge and of the fear of the LORD."**

Jesus, the mighty One of the tribe of Judah is able to open the scroll.

The Lamb received the book from the right hand of God which symbolized His power and authority. It contains God's entire plan of redemption and restoration until the end of human history. Because it is inscribed on both sides indicates that nothing remains to be added to it as it contains the complete will of the Father (see Revelation 22:18-19). Only the Lamb of God is entitled to open the seal to the history of salvation, which was foreshadowed in the Old Testament and put into action in the life of Jesus as well as in the early church. Now God's plan, which was sealed and hidden, can be revealed and fulfilled. Judgment has been entrusted to Him. The Lamb has also been given the authority to break the seven seals that no one else can break.

The New Song

In heaven we can see an awesome response to these events. The four living creatures and the twenty-four elders, each of whom hold a harp and golden censors filled with the prayers of the saints, fall prostrate before the Lamb, singing a new song to Him, **"You are worthy to take the scroll and to open its seals, because you were slain, and with your blood you purchased men for God from every tribe and language and people and nation. You have made them to be a kingdom and priests to serve our God, and they will reign on the earth"** (Revelation 5:9-10).

The new song was conceived in the hearts of the four living creatures and the twenty-four elders as they witnessed the events that were taking place in heaven. Upon the revelation of the sacrifice of Jesus and the life-changing grace for all mankind, they were singing a song of victory in praise of the cross because the rule of God and the priesthood of God's people had come. The Lamb opened up the pathway for the people of God to reign with Him.

Choirs of angels echoed the new song of the living creatures and the elders, proclaiming with a loud voice, **"Worthy is the Lamb, who was slain, to receive power and wealth and wisdom and strength and honor and glory and praise!"** (Revelation 5:12)

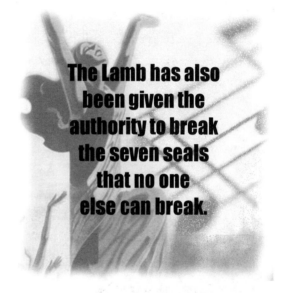

The Lamb has also been given the authority to break the seven seals that no one else can break.

This scene is quite similar to when the angel Gabriel announced the birth of Jesus to the shepherds. The heavenly hosts confirmed Gabriel's new song, joining in on the praises, **"Glory to God in the highest, and on earth peace to men on whom his favor rests"** (Luke 2:14).

Revelation 5 culminates in a remarkable crescendo of worship by a cosmic choir. Every creature joins in proclaiming, **"To him who sits on the throne and to the Lamb be praise and honor and glory** and power, for ever and ever!" The four living creatures said, "Amen," and the elders fell down and worshiped (Revelation 5:13-14).

The Son, represented by the Lamb of God who is being worshiped like the Father, has the same titles of honor attributed to Him. The will of the Father has come into being in heaven as well as on the earth!

We can now observe what "a new song" is and how it comes into being.

1. It focuses on God.

2. It is a reaction to something we have seen and/or heard or picked up in the Spirit.

3. It is a proclamation of a revelation of God's majesty, His workings, and His very being.

The will of the Father has come into being in heaven as well as on the earth!

Throughout history, there has been a constant stream of messages from the heart committed to music, such as Gregorian choruses, Handel's *Messiah*, Bach's Oratories and Cantatas, Haydn's creations, Mendelssohn's *Elijah*, and

Oliver Messiae's *Images of God* for the piano—just to name a few classics. Add to that the countless hymns that made an impact on generations after the Reformation and continue to do so to this day. How else could it be that Luther's, *A Mighty Fortress Is Our God* is currently experiencing such a revival in the Christian music scene and in many churches? Even in secular pop music, themes like love, faithfulness, pain, and loss are timeless, expressing basic human values and a deep longing for redemption and nobility.

In the more recent Christian music scene, waves of the stream can be detected. Some years ago, there was a strong emphasis on intimacy with Jesus. After that came a season of warfare and victory songs followed by the "Now Is the Time" era. Next, many songs were released about Jerusalem as the city of the great King being revered by all tribes and nations. I believe we are that currently seeing a new wave of evangelistic songs about healing and deliverance as well as a new song of unfeigned bridal love for Jesus, our Bridegroom.

The impact of a new song has been the same since the beginning. Many times, we will not have the slightest idea of what is being set in motion through the new songs that God places in our hearts. Nevertheless, the sound and energy they carry and the power of their words is being recorded in the heavens.

The New Sound

The new sound consists of several different noises as described by John in Revelation—the sound of many waters, mighty thunder, and harps. It is an attempt to capture and describe the sounds that make up the voices of the Father, the Son, and the Holy Spirit.

The voice of Jesus is depicted as the roaring of many waters (see Revelation 1:15). Breakers crashing on the seashore or the roaring of Niagara Falls might give us some hint of the mighty power of His voice.

The unleashed power of roaring thunderstorms is an eternal reminder of His majestic presence.

The voice of the Father is represented by thunder. The unleashed power of roaring thunderstorms is an eternal reminder of His majestic presence. When Jesus asked His Father to glorify His name, a voice came down from heaven, proclaiming, **"I have glorified it, and will glorify it again"** (John 12:28). The crowd who witnessed the scene **"said it had thundered" (John 12:29).** May God help us to grasp the meaning of the voice of thunder!

The voice of the Holy Spirit is represented by the sounds of harps, which is a symbol of eternal worship in and through the Holy Spirit. It is the sevenfold, perfect

worship in the diversity of the seven Spirits of God going from the throne room into the earth in order to spark the new song in all languages among all races and ethnic groups. The fact that there are many harps implies that this is not primarily a reference to individual worship but to the corporate worship of the body of Christ. Everything that separates and alienates, even that which is appalling because it is too noisy or quiet, must fall in line with the corporate song of worship inspired by the Spirit.

We cannot artificially produce that new sound. It will be birthed in us and grow as we come into a deeper knowledge of the Trinity. It comes into being when the worship in heaven and earth join each other.

So far, we have only seen a few examples of a choir of heavenly voices suddenly joining in on our "new songs" or of the noise of mighty waters joining in with the sound of our instruments. One thing is certain—just like the knowledge of God will fill the earth, the new sound will fill the earth. God is about to glorify Himself, beyond all limitations of form and style!

The Song of the Sealed Ones

"Then I looked, and there before me was the Lamb, standing on Mount Zion, and with Him 144,000 who had His name and His Father's name written on their foreheads.

And they sang a new song before the throne and before the four living creatures and the elders. No one could learn the song except the 144,000

who had been redeemed from the earth.

These are those who did not defile themselves with women, for they kept themselves pure. They follow the Lamb wherever He goes. They were purchased from among men and offered as firstfruits to God and the Lamb.

No lie was found in their mouths; they are blameless" (Revelation 14:1, 3-5).

Out of their love for God they have made up their minds to be obedient to God and His Word.

Mount Zion, on which the Lamb is standing, is not a geographical location but a spiritual one. Everyone belonging to Jesus has access to this place through the blood of the Lamb. It is the realm where eternal worship is already established; it is the seat of government, the city of God in heaven.

The 144,000 are the ones who are found faithful and who are sealed by the angels with the seal of the living God as described in Revelation 7:1-8. I believe the number 144,000 is a prophetic symbol for all those who are saved—1,000 being the number of a division in the army of Israel (see Numbers 31:4-5) and 12x12 the number of the faithful ones under the Old and New Covenants. The following are five characteristics which allow them to hear and learn the song of the Lamb:

1. They have the names of the Lamb and the name of the Father written on their foreheads. This is the sign that they no longer belong to or live for themselves but have been purchased through the blood of the Lamb and sealed by the Holy Spirit.

2. They are pure like virgins, which means they are spiritually pure. They have engaged themselves to the Lamb as their Bridegroom and have come to know the Lord (see Hosea 2:21-22). Their thoughts, emotions, and will are geared to pleasing the One they love. They did not bow their knees to Baal (see Romans 11:4), live in adultery, idolatry, or bow to the spirit of this age.

3. They follow the Lamb wherever He goes and have overcome by the love of God. Out of their love for God they have made up their minds to be obedient to God and His Word.

4. No lie can be found in their mouths. They proclaim life, promote hope, give comfort, encourage, lift up, and admonish (see I Corinthians 14:3). There is no discrepancy between what is in their hearts and what they profess.

5. They are above reproach. By faith they have taken hold of the reality that Jesus has become sin for them so they may be endowed with His righteousness. They know that only through Him are they able to live a life of truth, transparency, and holiness with the ability to admit mistakes and allow forgiveness and grace to flow.

The Song of Those Who Overcome

The song of the Lamb is also about those who overcome and honor the Father and the Lamb. Mentioned two times in Revelation 7 and 15 are specific groups of people who overcame.

Revelation 7:9-17 refers to a great multitude from all tribes and tongues and nations who are dressed in white robes as a sign of their righteousness. They are holding palm branches as a symbol of victory and of their tribute to Jesus. They have endured times of great tribulation and held on to their convictions, even in times of hardships. They overcame the evil one and made their robes spotless in the blood of the Lamb. They upheld their witness for Jesus, loving Him more than their own lives (see Revelation 12:11). Their lives are shining examples of the truth that no one can snatch us out of God's hand (see John 10:29).

To overcome means to hold on to our faith—no matter how high the costs—to put God and His kingdom first, to hope where there is no hope, and to trust God instead of focusing primarily on our circumstances. Many of those who went before us and have taken their places in the great cloud of witnesses, paid for their convictions with their lives. Think about the Anabaptists, the Huguenots, the martyrs of the eastern church, or the brothers and sisters in China and Pakistan. Their lives have become a victory song of those who overcome!

The Father Himself, the God of all comfort, will wipe away their tears.

I believe God is admonishing us to stand our ground as people who overcome. Those who overcome the great tribulation are allowed to serve God day and night. Neither hunger nor thirst will afflict them. No heat will bother them, for the Lamb is their Shepherd leading them to the sources of living water. The Father Himself, the God of all comfort, will wipe away their tears.

The second group is standing beside a sea of glass mixed with fire (see Revelation 15:2), which is a picture of the crystal clear foundation of the throne room in which the seven torches of the Spirit are burning. They are holding the harps of God in their hands. They received access to this place because they gained victory over the beast, its image, and the number of its name.

Here we see another secret at work. Those who overcome are standing in this place because they held on to the Word of truth and the righteousness of God. They did not fight by their own means, but used the harp of God as their weapon. They overcame by their praise and worship. The song of the Lamb and their worship in Spirit and truth saved them from becoming worshipers and followers of the beast.

The song of the Lamb will ultimately turn into a wedding song!

Those who overcome sing **"the song of Moses the servant of God and the song of the Lamb" (Revelation 15:3).** The song of these two fighters for freedom culminates in worship of God and ends with the prophetic proclamation that all people will come to worship Him.

Great and marvelous are your deeds, Lord God Almighty. Just and true are your ways, King of the ages.

Who will not fear you, O Lord, and bring glory to your name? For you alone are holy.

All nations will come and worship before you, for your righteous acts have been revealed (Revelation 15:3-4).

The Song of the Bride

The song of the Lamb will ultimately turn into a wedding song! The bride, the universal church of the ones belonging to Jesus, will celebrate her wedding with the Lamb of God. **"Blessed are those who are invited to the wedding supper of the Lamb!" (Revelation 19:9)** All of us are called to be part of it; each one of us has received His invitation. The preparations for the wedding are in full swing.

How the Melodies of our Lives Become the Song of the Lamb

The book of Revelation attributes special importance to the new song of the Lamb. We are living in the final period of history, the time of labor pains, and God intends for all of the challenges and afflictions to draw us ever closer to Him. Thus, the melodies of our lives will be turned into the song of the Lamb.

The new song is more than a lifestyle of forgiveness and praise—it the song of the Lamb—the restoring power of God is working in and through us in heaven and on earth. Are we willing to live the song of those who overcome, loving the truth, justice, and righteousness of God more than our own lives?

If that is so then the love song of the Lamb will be birthed in us over and over again, as individuals and corporately. The bridal church will then sing, "Maranatha! Come, Lord Jesus! Come soon!" ∎

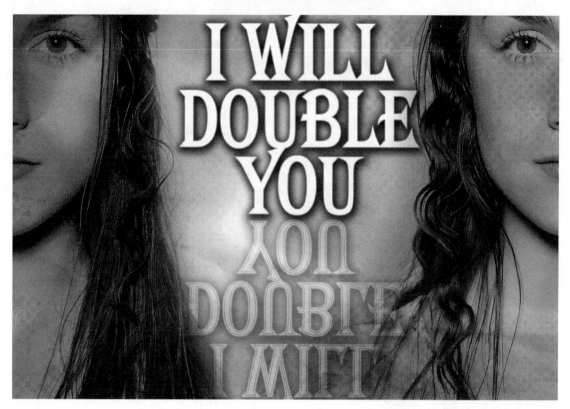

I WILL DOUBLE YOU

by Francis Frangipane

Much of the work God does when guiding us to our destiny unfolds in our lives unnoticed until the time of its manifestation. Seemingly insignificant aspects of our lives suddenly bloom into profound realities, filling our consciousness with the fragrance of the Lord's presence. The natural is transformed by the supernatural, leaving us forever changed.

These "God-moments" reveal that the Lord has been intimately aware of us, and long before we recognized Him, He was working in our lives. I have told this story before, but it is worth repeating. It was in the spring of 1971 when I had a most significant encounter with the Lord. It was at this time that He first spoke to me of my future. It began with a life-changing dream. In the midst of great darkness, the Lord revealed that there would be a great outpouring of the Holy Spirit. The next morning, as I contemplated the vision, I read Isaiah 60:1-3 and then Matthew 14 for the first time in my young Christian life. Both of these texts confirmed in dramatic detail the truth of my night vision. The Isaiah text spoke of nations coming to Christ, while Matthew's story chronicled Jesus feeding the multitudes with the bread and fish.

The God-moment peaked as I read that Jesus had blessed and broken the bread. Suddenly, it occurred to me that my last name, Frangipane, actually means "to break bread." Throughout my life this long last name had been a nuisance. Yet now, coupled with the dream and the promise from Isaiah, the story of Christ taking "broken bread" to feed multitudes became a personal encouragement to me. Later that morning, I related the vision and the Lord's promise from Isaiah 60 to my wife, Denise. I then told her about the feeding of the five thousand, mentioning that God would use us like Jesus used the loaves and fish to feed the multitudes. I also explained that Frangipane, in fact, means "to break bread." Since she now had my last name, God had included her in my calling. In childlike wonder, she replied that this destiny would not only be about me. She then informed me of the meaning of her maiden name, Piscitelli, which means "little fishes."

Those Whom He Foreknew

The fact that the Lord would quietly orchestrate our lives, and then confirm His promise in the very meaning of our names still fills our souls with awe. I imagine that a similar sense of awe struck King Josiah when, as a young man, he discovered his name in the Scriptures. Indeed, his kingship had been foretold 350 years previously by a prophet in Israel; the man of God even described the actual tasks Josiah would fulfill (see I Kings 13:2). The revelation of having been foreknown by God caused Josiah to become, perhaps, the most zealous of all of Israel's kings.

This same awe must have struck King Cyrus of Persia when he discovered that the God of Israel had foretold of his leadership by name 150 years prior to his birth (see Isaiah 44:28). The knowledge that we have been predestined by God to accomplish great things for Him, that He actually calls His sheep by name, adds great zeal to our souls.

Certainly David must have felt this awe when he wrote the following:

O LORD, **You have searched me and known me.**

You know when I sit down and when I rise up; You understand my thought from afar.

You scrutinize my path and my lying down, and are intimately acquainted with all my ways

Even before there is a word on my tongue, behold, O LORD, **You know it all.**

You have enclosed me behind and before, and laid Your hand upon me.

Such knowledge is too wonderful for me; it is too high, I cannot attain to it (Psalm 139:1-6).

Even at this very moment the Holy Spirit continues to work in you His predetermined plan.

Whether or not your name has a significant meaning in it, however, is not the issue. You are significant. God chose you in Christ before the foundation of the world; He has written your name in heaven (see Ephesians 1:4; Revelation 21:27). Even at this very moment the Holy Spirit continues to work in you His predetermined plan. At the proper time, the miracle of God's activity will emerge in your life like clockwork. ■

Stranded in the Will of God

by Suzanne Hirt

I was soaring on the back of a giant eagle, the wind racing through my hair, and blood coursing through my veins like a surge of electricity. I was not afraid, but this was certainly not like anything I had ever experienced. This eagle was on a mission and I was along for the ride. We soon came in sight of a mountain range and flew swiftly and directly to one particular mountain, entering into its core. The mountain was inhabited by ghost-like people, trapped in a state of perpetual slumber. These living dead were desensitized to their lifeless spiritual state and to the world around them, but the eagle had come with a purpose.

With me still on his back, overcome with awe and curiosity, he began to flap his wings, slowly at first, then faster and faster until the countenances of the people started to transform and become clear. The wind of the Spirit stirred up by the eagle was a breath of life to their dark, decaying forms. They came alive with joy and passion once again, a mighty army liberated from apathy's deadly grip. Equipped with new vision and purpose, these soldiers set out individually for various destinations and callings. A few of the soldiers climbed onto the eagle's back with me.

The Deserted Island

The eagle, with no doubt as to his destination, once again took flight. We ascended high above the landscape and were soon over the open sea. We flew a great distance out over the middle of the ocean with no land visible in any direction. At last, a small deserted island came into view and we drifted down to alight on its beach. We climbed off of the eagle's back and he, without warning, took to the air again and was soon out of sight. I suddenly realized I had a sword strapped to my side. With no discussion about why the eagle had stranded us on the island or what purpose the experience might serve, we tried using our swords to chop down trees, hoping to build a raft from their trunks on which to escape this seemingly God-forsaken spit of land in the center of nowhere.

> In Christ we find our provision, our strength, our daily bread.

At this point in my third heaven adventure, the Lord came to me with wisdom and revelation on the meaning of this strange experience. He told me that we were not to build a raft, but a residence. He promised the eagle would return when it was time. It was His will for me to be here; He had set aside this time for training and preparation, to accomplish a specific purpose in my life. The eagle, the island, and the seclusion of this place all began to make sense.

The Lord designs prophetic seasons in our lives, times of trial and rigorous training. He sets us down in the middle of what, to our natural minds, appears to be a deserted island. We think the Lord has abandoned us, forgetting His promise in the Word that the steps of the righteous are ordered by the Lord. It seems that everything in our lives is changing so we concentrate all of our mental energy into searching for a plan of escape, a way out of our troubles, a raft to flee our deserted island. We have not been forsaken; the Lord is with us and He is whispering direction to our hearts. If we will turn our efforts from building a raft to building a residence, the Lord will guide us through the difficult season. To build a residence on a deserted island is to embrace one's plight, living in the moment while preparing for the future.

Partake of His Food and Drink

During this island experience, the Lord shared with me several keys for turning trials into training. When we finished building our residence, He placed two barrels inside, one filled with food and the other with drink. He said that all we needed to sustain us during this time was contained in those two barrels; we were not to partake of food or drink from any other source. Even in the harshest conditions, the Lord provides us with all we need to endure. We are to eat of His body and drink of His blood. Communion with Him, time spent in His presence, gives us the nourishment we need to walk through our valleys. In Christ we find our provision, our strength, our daily bread.

Get Fit and Ready

The Lord's next instruction was to sharpen our swords daily and practice all the maneuvers one uses in sword fighting. I was reminded of a scene from the recent film *The Last Samurai*. The samurai warriors spent hours every day honing their skills. They went through every thrust of the sword, every defensive block hundreds of times. They trained intensely during the winter months so that when spring arrived, the season for going to battle, they would be fit and ready. Hebrews 4:12 compares the Word of God to a sword. We sharpen this sword by meditating on the Word until it becomes a part of us, engraved on the tablets of our hearts. When we have sharpened our spirit in this way, we will be able to cut down thoughts planted by the enemy with the Word that lives in us. We will not always have access to a Bible or time to search out an applicable Scripture in a crisis; it is the living Word within us that defeats the enemy.

The next key the Lord shared was to run around the island every day at high tide when the water covered its sandy beaches. Running in this capacity would increase our endurance and help us shed any excess weight we had taken on. Choosing to take the hard route would help us stay in good spiritual shape. Taking the easy road keeps us lazy and only leads to a lesser reward. The high path is rarely the path of least resistance; it is the way of the cross. Every time we choose the cross instead of the easy road, we shake off some of the spiritual baggage that weighs us down so as to run the race set before us more effectively.

Trust the Lord's Provision

Another revelation the Lord gave me was to practice flying, high up around the perimeter of the island so we could see any possible threat while it was yet far off. This came as quite a surprise because I had not known we were capable of flying. My mind was churning with possibilities. If we could fly, we could get off this island and I could go back to the way things were before all this began to unfold. The Lord knew my thoughts and simply asked, "Where will you go? Do you know the way?" Of course I had no idea which direction pointed homeward so I ceased my scheming and listened to His wisdom. Even after the Lord had revealed all that I was to accomplish while I was here, my first response to learning I possessed this great gift of flight was to use it to escape my circumstances. The Lord gives us more than we need to make it through our trials; He gives us spiritual gifts. We selfishly use His provision for our own purposes and agendas. The Lord had enabled us to fly so we could be watchmen and see any enemy that gathered on the horizon. The Lord grants us spiritual insight and discernment of what is coming so we will be prepared for the enemy and not be taken out by surprise attacks. We fail to trust the Lord when we try to escape the circumstances into which He places us by flying away.

Engage the Lord

The Lord advised us to keep our island camouflaged so that an enemy passing overhead would not be aware of our presence on the island. We were to take care of our swords and not leave them lying around unattended. They were to stay on our person at all times. The Lord warned us not to engage the enemy; if we saw an enemy lurking close to our island, we were to stay hidden in the brush. He said to lay low because it was not the time to attack. It seems that when we find ourselves in a trial, we immediately begin rebuking demons and exhausting ourselves in warfare when, in reality, the Lord is the author of our difficulties. Instead of entering into unnecessary skirmishes, we need to make the most of our trials. We must use our time and energy to engage the Lord rather than the enemy. The Lord told us above all to ask for His heart. Our time on the island was to be used for getting in shape, gaining strength, and increasing our endurance.

In parting, the Lord said He was teaching our hands to war. Learning the art of war is part of the Lord's purpose during our trials. He is seeking to change our mentality about how to do battle with the enemy. We have a distorted concept, a Cain-type mindset that we have to produce results, working and striving to bring about God's purpose when the truth is we do greater damage to the devil when we simply worship and become more like Christ.

Embrace the Island

Through my prophetic experience of being stranded on a deserted island, I saw that my typical reaction to trials has been to try to make things happen for myself, to put forth my best effort to escape the situation and get back on the right path, according to my own idea of the right path. The will of God for our lives is for us to be changed into His image and His plan is often perfected in times of crisis. I mistakenly, though with the best of intentions, believe I will be better off if I fly away back to the mountaintop where

life is good and I feel the Lord again. I am wasting my trials by having this frame of mind. In my pain and difficulty, Christ Himself is taking over, completing His work within me. All my desperate attempts at freedom are comparable to running a race on a treadmill, exhausting my resources for a fruitless cause.

To make the most of our trials we must embrace the island, accept our circumstances, and permit the Lord to teach our hands to war in a new, unconventional way we are not accustomed to. If we allow Him this liberty in our lives, we will have to follow His instructions for life on the island. We will have no choice but to partake only of His flesh and drink His blood. We will have to feed on His Word until it becomes a part of us, continually sharpened like a fiery sword. We must allow our hearts to be replaced with His heart.

Conclusion

Every place the Lord takes us, every obstacle, valley, or island is for one purpose. The Lord wants to inhabit our lives. Every trial cuts away more of our personal agendas and thinking patterns. If we were fully possessed by Him we would have His thoughts, feelings, and desires. We would see people through His eyes and understand His ways. We have all had a deserted island experience and will probably have many more of them. When we find ourselves on another island, let us open wide our hearts, build a residence, and dwell there until the Lord's purpose in that season is complete, forsaking our vain labors so that our spirits may become one with the Spirit of God. ∎

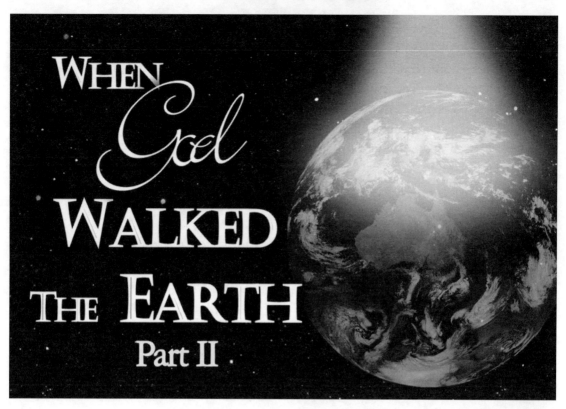

WHEN God WALKED THE EARTH
Part II

by Rick Joyner

Andrew awoke first. It took him a minute to get his bearings in the unfamiliar surroundings. When he saw John, he remembered Jesus with a start. Quickly looking around the little cottage, and not seeing Him, he shook John to wake him up.

"Wake up, John. Where is He? Did you see Him leave?"

John quickly sat up, wiping his eyes. Then the events of the previous days came cascading down upon his still sleepy mind. Glancing around the tiny cottage, John almost shouted:

"Where is He? Did you see Him leave?"

"That's what I just asked you!" Andrew shot back. "Let's go find Him."

After they quickly gathered their belongings, put on their sandals, and wrapped themselves in their simple shawls, they started to bolt through the door just as Jesus opened it.

"Good morning," He said, glancing at them. "You seem to have slept well."

Backing up to let Him in, John was the first to reply,

"We were just going to look for you," and then added after an awkward pause, "I trust you also slept well. I hope we did not bother you too much with all of our questions last night."

"No. You did not bother Me with too many questions. I enjoy your zeal. Here, I have brought you some bread," Jesus said, handing each of them a loaf.

"Sir, you should have sent us out to get bread," Andrew mumbled, embarrassed to think that he had slept while the One John indicated to be Messiah, had gone out to get bread for them.

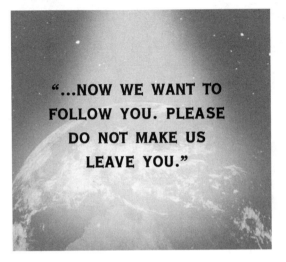

"...NOW WE WANT TO FOLLOW YOU. PLEASE DO NOT MAKE US LEAVE YOU."

Jesus seemed to disregard Andrew's remark and continued. "After we eat, I must go to be alone for a few weeks, and you must return to your homes."

Stunned, John quickly interjected, "Master, we have followed the Baptist for many months and now we want to follow You. Please do not make us leave You."

Jesus looked up at them and asked patiently, "Do you not miss your families?"

John and Andrew looked at each other and then John answered, "Yes. We do miss them. But there are sacrifices one must make to do the will of God."

"This is true," the Lord responded, "but not all sacrifices are His will."

John and Andrew both pondered this for a moment before John continued. "After being with the Baptist we will never be satisfied with normal lives again. And now that we know who You are, how can we return to our families? We love them, but we could never return to the life we had before."

Beckoning them to sit, Jesus continued, "I understand, but I must go away alone for a time, however, I will return for you. Until I do, please enjoy your families. You will make many sacrifices to follow Me, but I have come to sacrifice for the sake of families. You must enjoy yours when you can."

Andrew and John were visibly relieved. They knew that when He said He would return for them it meant they were accepted as His disciples. They both watched Him as He sat and began giving thanks for their bread.

As the three sat talking, the captains who watched over them listened to every word. They were still amazed at how casual these two men were with the Son, and how casual He was with them. The stars sang His praise and millions of angels did His bidding, yet on this little speck of dust called "earth," no one recognized Him. Even more amazing, He seemed to enjoy being on such a casual basis with these people. This was something they had never seen in heaven, nor even considered possible.

As a messenger angel approached them, the two captains turned to receive him. To their astonishment, it was Gabriel himself. They both bowed low on one knee and saluted with their swords, as did the thousands of warriors arrayed about them.

"Greetings. I have come with your orders. Each of you are to take your host and remain with these two men. They will be parting from the Lord for a time and you must watch over them. Michael will stay with the Lord."

"Yes, sir. We will watch the two. Michael talked with us last night and we assumed that he would remain with the Lord."

TO THEIR ASTONISHMENT, IT WAS GABRIEL HIMSELF.

The captains still had a look of astonishment on their faces as they looked at Gabriel, so he continued, "I know you are wondering why I came. It is true that I do not come to the earth unless there is the beginning of a new age and that is why I am here now."

"Sir," the other captain replied, "you just came to speak to the virgin, so why are you back so soon? Is another age beginning already? It does not seem that this one is yet complete."

"True," Gabriel replied. "When the Son came to earth it was the beginning of a new age. The entire creation now has its attention on this little planet. But another age for man began only two days ago. The Son will not be here much longer, but the age which has just begun will last as long as the earth."

All of the angels in the area were keenly listening as Gabriel spoke, and he looked about to be sure that they would all know he was speaking to them, too.

"When the Son went down to the prophet John to be baptized, you saw the Holy Spirit come and remain upon Him. He came in the form of a dove as a symbol of the dove that Noah released from the ark, which did not return to him. Man could not find his rest until the Holy Spirit returned to rest on Him. The Son is the first man whom the Holy Spirit has been able to descend upon and remain, finding rest. There will be others with whom the Spirit will be able to remain, many of whom are now being born. When the Spirit can rest upon men, men will then begin to find their rest in God. Then man will be restored to God."

"This is unfathomable!" one of the captains replied as the entire company of angels who were standing by shifted noticeably.

"Yes. The Son has become a man to begin preparing men who can receive the Holy Spirit."

"Sir," the captain continued in a tone of protest, "we heard the message given to the Baptist that he was to prepare the way for the One who would baptize with the Holy Spirit, but how can the Holy Spirit remain upon men...other than the Son, of course?"

"Good captain, I understand your question, but I am afraid that even I do not fully know the answer. I do know that when the Son accomplishes His work here, men will begin to change. Many will become vessels in whom the Holy Spirit will be able to abide. Men will become the dwelling place of God. Looking at them now, it is very hard to understand, but they were actually created for this."

"I have seen how the Holy Spirit loves men and loves being with them, even though they are so contrary to His nature," one of the captains interjected. "Even though He is holy and they are so wicked, He always seems to be looking for an opportunity to get close to them and to help them. There is obviously a special love between the Spirit and men.

Looking at the two disciples, Gabriel replied, "Watching Him has helped me to love both men and God even more. I, for one, am very happy for men, even if it is beyond my understanding of how He will ever be able to make His dwelling place with them. We are all learning a lot about our God as we learn about men. The virgin, who carried the Son, brought such joy to the Holy Spirit. She has also been such a delight to the Son since He has been here. Even if it is a great mystery to us, it is wonderful to see their joy in men. There is such darkness and evil here it is a marvel when any of them turn to the light. Those who do become a special delight to God."

THERE IS OBVIOUSLY A SPECIAL LOVE BETWEEN THE SPIRIT AND MEN.

"You understand much," Jesus said, as if He had been involved in the entire conversation. Gabriel, the captains, and the entire host knelt, bowed their heads and drew their swords in a salute that caused the entire mountainside to glisten with a fiery glory.

Michael was standing with Him as He gazed over the host and then toward John and Andrew who were just beginning to walk down the narrow road. As Michael nodded toward the two, the host began falling in behind them. Other companies of hundreds began taking positions over them or in front of them. The procession was more magnificent than any that Caesar had ever beheld for himself, yet John and Andrew were completely unaware of it.

"These did not choose Me, but My Father chose them, even before the foundation of this world," Jesus explained to Gabriel and the captains. "They are two of the elect. They are My brothers. Treat them as you would Me."

"Thank You for this honor of serving Your brethren," the first captain replied as the other nodded his agreement.

"I know you will do well," Jesus replied as He began to walk down the road in the opposite direction of the two.

Suddenly the mountains themselves seemed to disappear in a great flash of light as Michael drew his sword. Instantly, a great host of mighty warrior angels appeared, all of whom seemed equal to the captains in power. Their swords were drawn and the fierce glory emanating from them was a spectacle not often witnessed beyond the inner sanctuary of heaven itself. The captains who followed Andrew and John were briefly stunned before instinctively drawing their own swords. Angels throughout the realm, in all of the little towns and villages, all likewise drew their swords and stood as if ready for battle.

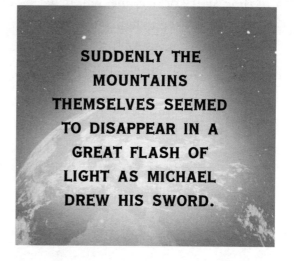

SUDDENLY THE MOUNTAINS THEMSELVES SEEMED TO DISAPPEAR IN A GREAT FLASH OF LIGHT AS MICHAEL DREW HIS SWORD.

"I had no idea there were so many of us here," one of the captains exclaimed to his companion.

"Neither did I," said the other. "But why the alarm…?"

As his words tapered off, they both knew the reason. A terrible cloud was coming from the direction of the sea. This could be none other than the entourage of the evil one himself. As the cloud grew closer, great storms arose and began to thrash the coastal villages.

"Why does he delight in tormenting men like that? Look at him sending lightning to hit those little shacks, and kicking up waves to turn over those boats. He will not intimidate us that way. The power of Michael's sword alone could destroy him, and we could easily dispense of his entire host," the captain shouted as the evil clamor grew."

"He can flaunt the authority that he now has over the earth, but the time will soon come when we will be allowed to fight," the other captain reminded him. "But I believe he knows he cannot intimidate us. He simply hates men and delights in smiting them like that because he knows they think that God is doing it. He tries to make them think God hates them so that they will not seek Him."

> WHEN WE GAVE MAN THE FREEDOM IN THE GARDEN TO OBEY OR DISOBEY, WE GAVE HIM THE FREEDOM TO CHOOSE HIS OWN MASTER.

The angels in the villages now had their hands full guarding their new charges from the host of demons released among them. There were many clashes, but the demons quickly learned not to touch the elect. Enraged, they charged off after men and women who were not protected.

Terrible fights broke out in a multitude of homes. Demons of lust jumped on men, women, and children, causing more than a few to stumble that night. Insanity and fear attached themselves to others, aided by the atmosphere created from the storm. It was the beginning of a most unholy night in the land called "holy."

Michael drew next to Jesus as He walked. "Master, can we do nothing?"

"My heart breaks too, good friend. I know that you have watched over My people Israel for many centuries and have witnessed many such attacks by the enemy. I know the test that it is for you not to respond. The day will come when you can, and you will be the bearer of the vengeance of God, but this is not the time.

When we gave man the freedom in the Garden to obey or disobey, we gave him the freedom to choose his own master. I am here to give men another chance to choose, and the choice will be more clear now that they have known the consequences of disobedience. But before I can help them I must walk in obedience as a man. Then I will be able to show them the way out of this terrible darkness. Even then not all will choose Me. But even if just a few return to My Father, it will be worth what I am here to do."

"But why has the evil one left Rome to come here?" Michael inquired.

"He has come to tempt Me just as he did the first Adam," the Lord replied.

"Master, I know You can dispense of him at will. How does he have the nerve to tempt You like that?"

"When I face him it will not be as the Son of God, but as the Son of man. I must do what the first Adam did not do. I must remain faithful. My Father gave this world to man to rule over it, and a man must take back the authority by obeying in all things. I am that man. That is why I must face him as a man and not as God."

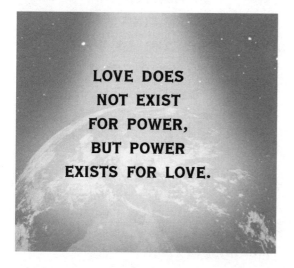

LOVE DOES NOT EXIST FOR POWER, BUT POWER EXISTS FOR LOVE.

"I understand," the archangel replied. "I have understood that for a long time, but it is still so hard for us to restrain ourselves when we could dispense of him and his evil host so easily."

"I did not come to win back the world with power, but with love," Jesus continued.

"Those who resort to power first will misuse their power. Love does not exist for power, but power exists for love. Not understanding this was part of what caused the evil one to fall. What I am doing here is not just for man, but for the whole creation.

For all of eternity the creation will study what I do here, and it will keep many others from falling as Lucifer did."

"Though it was hard for all of us to watch him rebel the way he did, it was even more difficult to see You let him go forth to recruit for his rebellion without stopping him," Michael admitted. "It was a very confusing time for us all, but we have known Your goodness, and we just had to trust You."

Jesus stopped for a minute and looked the great angel in the eyes. "The love of power will always lead to a fall. Only when we use power for love's sake will we use it rightly. I am not here to reveal power, but love. You know how easy it would be for Me to stop the sun like I did for Joshua or even part the Great Sea, but this would so overwhelm men that they would choose Me out of fear, whether they loved the truth or loved Me or not. I will only use enough power to reveal My love for them. I do not want men to choose Me because of power, but because they love Me and love the truth. I will not be known as Power, but as Truth, and Love."

"Master, Your ways are marvelous beyond our comprehension. All of the angels in heaven are growing in wisdom as we behold Your deeds here," the great angel replied, his eyes glistening with emotion like a man's. "You have entrusted me with great power and great authority, but I value beholding Your ways even more than my power. I treasure being able to feel love as I do now. Watching You causes me to grow in love, too. I can now say that I want to fight for these men because I love them, not just because I despise the enemy, but I still want to respond with power at times."

"You are a wise servant, My friend," Jesus replied. "You were all brought forth with a purpose, and the power that has been given to you will be fully used. But you must always remember that for it to be rightly used, you must use it in love. Even when you are released to fight and destroy the evil ones, you must do it for the right reasons, which you are learning here. But now you must wait here and let Me go on alone."

The archangel stopped, but with obvious protest in his eyes. "Master…"

"It must be this way," the Lord replied. "I must go into this desert alone. You and your host must wait here."

Jesus walked on into the desert, under a cloud of darkness like had never been witnessed on the earth before. Demons of every kind were swarming through the mid-heavens all around and above the wilderness. The presence of the evil one himself was felt by the angels throughout the region, though he was not seen because of the great swarming darkness around him. No angel for a thousand miles would sheath his sword for the next forty days.

ALL OF THE ANGELS IN HEAVEN ARE GROWING IN WISDOM AS WE BEHOLD YOUR DEEDS HERE.

Several captains drew close to Michael, bowed and saluted. For a few minutes he did not even seem to notice them, and then he beckoned them to come forward.

"Sir, what shall we do?" one of them asked.

"Stand at the ready, guard your charges, but do not attack," Michael replied, still looking in the direction Jesus had disappeared.

"Never have we seen the enemy gather like this," one of the other captains replied.

"You are new here, aren't you?" the archangel asked turning to look at the captain who spoke.

"Yes sir. I have come from a far galaxy. I was sent here to watch over one of the elect who was just born today. I am so honored to get this commission, but it is already a little more exciting than I was expecting. Is this the beginning of the last battle?"

"None of us knows the time of the last battle, but what I do know makes me think that it is yet many seasons from now. The elect whom you have been sent to watch will be mighty champions who will themselves prevail over the evil one. They will fight with a power greater than we angels possess, yet now most are still infants and many are even yet to be born."

"How can that be?" several of the captains responded with obvious shock. "They do not have even as much power as the least of the messenger angels. In fact, they do not seem to have much power in their own natural realm, insignificant even when compared to the beasts," one of them continued.

"They will be given the power of the Holy Spirit," Michael responded. "When the Holy Spirit comes to abide in them they will

have more power than all of us together. The power that created us, and the heavens themselves, will be in even the least of them."

A great hush fell over the entire group of captains, which now numbered in the hundreds. This was incomprehensible to them. Finally, one ventured another question.

> THE ELECT WHOM YOU HAVE BEEN SENT TO WATCH WILL BE MIGHTY CHAMPIONS WHO WILL THEMSELVES PREVAIL OVER THE EVIL ONE.

"How can the Holy Spirit abide in these who are so unholy? I have only been here a few months and I have seen more evil in these men than I knew existed and that is even in the best of them! It is hard for me to understand how the Holy Spirit touched even the prophets as briefly as He did to give them words and visions, but to abide in these..."

"I understand your questions, but I also know that somehow the Son is here to make men holy again. They will behold His glory and be changed. They will see His love and be purified. There is a power in His love that we have a hard time understanding, but these men will understand it. They will love Him with a great love because He will deliver them from so much. The great love that is about to be revealed by Him is greater than any power we have known before. It is so great that the time will come when we will all marvel more over the love that He reveals here than we did over the power we saw released to create the stars."

There was a long silence as the host of captains pondered this. Finally, one of them spoke, "Why did the Son walk into that desert alone? And why does the evil one and his host not flee before Him?"

"If He lifted His finger they would all flee. But He said that He must face the evil one as a man. He will not violate His own decrees. This world was given to man to rule, and man gave himself to the evil one. The Son has come as a man to win back this world with His obedience."

Hesitating to let this sink in, the great commander continued, "As hard as this is to comprehend, even when He has won back this world as a man, He will not force men to return to Him. If He uses His power alone to turn men back to Him, He said that there would still be disobedience in their hearts.

Then they could never become true worshipers."

"The time will come when He will use His power, and we will be allowed to use ours, but first He wants to gather those who love truth more than power. These are the heirs. Those who come because of His power will become subjects, but they will not be joint heirs like those who come because they love Him and love His truth."

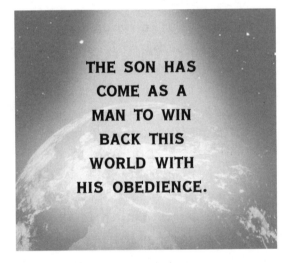

THE SON HAS COME AS A MAN TO WIN BACK THIS WORLD WITH HIS OBEDIENCE.

"His ways are more marvelous than we have ever comprehended," offered one of the captains. "Yes," Michael replied. "When man chose to disobey in the Garden, and the wickedness of men's hearts grew as deep as it did in the days of Noah, how badly we all just wanted to destroy this little planet along with the evil one and his hosts. We just could not understand why the

Lord was so patient with these little creatures. Now we are seeing a glory in His ways that is so wonderful that even we are constantly being changed and matured to love our God more than ever. These are both terrible and wonderful times."

John walked into his home for the first time in many months. The servants came running, calling to his mother that he had returned. Joy filled the house and was heard at the dock where James and his father were working on one of their boats. They knew what the commotion was about even before the servant reached them with the news. Smiling to each other, they arose and began walking to the house.

John flung his arms around his father while reaching over to knock his brother's hat off of his head. A good natured wrestling match was about to begin until Zebedee restrained them.

"Son, we have missed you, more than you can imagine."

"I'm sorry, Father. I did not mean to be gone so long. But such wonderful things have been happening, I simply could not leave. I have so much to tell you. These are the times that our people have been waiting so many centuries for."

"Son, we want to hear all about it. But first, you must wash and change your clothes. We are going to have a feast to celebrate your return."

"Thank you, Father," John replied, hugging his mother again. "It's so good to be back here with you."

Giving his brother a big shove, John departed for his room, determined to wash and return as quickly as he could. Joy was flooding his soul. He felt as if he were the most blessed man alive—to have such a family, to have had the experience of being taught by the Baptist, and then to have found the Messiah. He was bursting to tell every detail to his family, but he knew the rules of the house. Dinner was the time for such conversation, which is why their dinners usually lasted several hours.

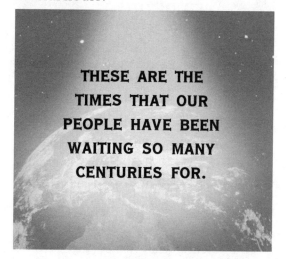

THESE ARE THE TIMES THAT OUR PEOPLE HAVE BEEN WAITING SO MANY CENTURIES FOR.

It had been quiet for a few minutes. Finally Zebedee spoke up. "You're sure this man is the Messiah? We have heard so much about the Baptist, and I was sure when I heard him myself that he is a prophet. I am so thankful that he would accept you as a disciple, but you know so little about this other man. Are you sure that you heard the Baptist right. Is 'the Lamb of God' the same as the Messiah?"

James had said nothing, but was watching his brother's every expression. To him, too, it seemed that John may have been a little too hasty to leave the extraordinary opportunity of being one of the Baptist's disciples since he knew so little about this other man.

MY GREATEST JOY HAS BEEN TO SEE MY SONS BECOME SO DEVOTED TO HIM.

"Sir," John answered, carefully looking at his father, "I know that you think I may have been too quick to leave the Baptist, but if you had been there...if you had heard the voice we heard...and then heard what the Baptist said about Him.

"He said that his whole life had been a preparation for that one day. He said that now Jesus would increase and he would begin to decrease."

As the family reclined at dinner, all of the servants had come to sit around the room and listen. They were all friends as well as servants, and Zebedee wanted them to all enjoy the celebration for John's return.

"Son," Zebedee continued, "I have watched you on your quest to know God from the time you were very small. I, too, have tried to serve Him all of my life. My greatest joy has been to see my sons become so devoted to Him. He has been good to me, and I know that He will be good to you. I am sure that He will lead you in His ways. But after so many centuries, to believe that the Messiah could really be here... it just seems too wonderful to contemplate."

Finally James spoke up, "Good brother, I know you well enough to believe that this Jesus is at least another prophet and maybe even one greater than John. For Him to be the Lamb . . . well, I just am not sure what that means, and I am surely not ready to say that He is the Messiah. But I must confess that John's testimony of Him must be taken seriously. I also know John often said that he was preparing the way for the Messiah. Maybe they are the same, the Lamb and the Messiah. You're sure that this man said He would come for you in a few weeks?"

"That is what He said. But I am embarrassed to say in the intensity of the moment I neglected to tell

Him where I lived. However, He knew that I had a family, and that I needed to return to spend some time with you, and I am sure that I did not tell Him anything about you, so maybe He even knows where I live."

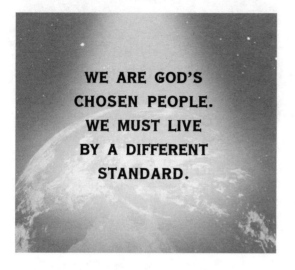

WE ARE GOD'S CHOSEN PEOPLE. WE MUST LIVE BY A DIFFERENT STANDARD.

"If He is a prophet, I guess He will find you," James offered with a snicker.

"I sure hope so," John replied, a little nervously.

"Well, I think it is time to retire," Zebedee said, rising. "Those storms a couple of nights ago did a lot of damage. It will take us weeks to repair some of the boats and nets. And we were fortunate compared to some of our neighbors. I've never seen such storms come up so quickly. It was as if the wrath of God was being unleashed upon us. We must deserve it. There must have been a dozen adulteries exposed in the nation last year, and now with what Herod is

doing...There seems to be an unending assault on the family."

"Father, why would God judge us so severely when the rest of the nations are so much worse?" James half asked and half stated. "That does not seem right to me."

"Because we are God's chosen people. We must live by a different standard. He has given us more truth so He expects us to be different," Zebedee retorted, a little forcefully as if they had had the same conversation before.

John listened carefully, pondering every comment deeply. He resolved to ask Jesus about these things. The way He had answered all of their questions the night they stayed with Him still amazed him. He saw everything from a perspective that was far above anything he had heard from the teachers of the Law. Certainly He would know the answer to James' question. The very thought thrilled John. The Baptist had once called Jesus "the Son of God." To think of being taught about God by God Himself! That was too much for even John to fathom for very long.

Peter was trying to be patient with his brother. He was very glad to see him, but he was also quite agitated that he had been gone for so long, leaving their fishing business when he was needed the most, now, with their only boat having sunk in the storm. But Andrew did not even seem to care.

"I'm happy for you to have found the Messiah, but we had better think about trying to find where our next meal is going to come from," Peter finally blurted out.

Andrew was a little stunned and then he looked around at the mess that was still left over from the storm. "Of course. Please forgive me, Peter. I have not even asked you how things have been going. I heard about the storm and the boat as I came into town. You have a wife and family to think about. I can understand why you were worried. I'll be here for a while and will help get things going again."

"You mean you will be leaving again?" Peter asked, furrowing his brow in what Andrew knew was his most irritated gesture.

"Peter, I must. How can I not follow the Messiah? We, as a people, have lived for this time."

Peter spun around to look out over the sea. They both stood in silence for a few minutes, and then Peter spoke, "You're right, my brother. I know that we have spent centuries as a people waiting for Him, but I would just like to hear about one person who gets a prayer answered! I have tried my whole life to be obedient. I go to the synagogue every Sabbath. I work hard for my family. Why does God then do this to us?"

Andrew knew better than to try to answer these questions. Finally he stepped over to his brother, wrapped an arm around his shoulders, and pulled him toward the house. "Come, I must see your

wife and children. How I have missed them all. Everything will work out. It always does. Nothing will hold you down for long. It will just give the fish a chance to get a little bigger before we catch them!"

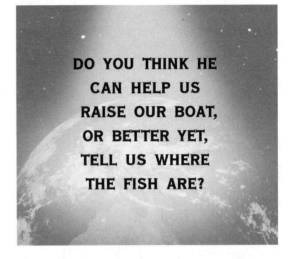

DO YOU THINK HE CAN HELP US RAISE OUR BOAT, OR BETTER YET, TELL US WHERE THE FISH ARE?

"It is good to see you, brother," Peter said, finally smiling. "Only, I do not like to hear about you leaving again."

"I know. But we will have plenty of time to talk about it. The Rabbi will not be coming for me for several weeks."

"What? He's coming here?"

"Yes. He said that He would come for me in a few weeks."

"Very good. I have never met a Messiah," Peter retorted with a chuckle. "Do you think He can help us raise our boat, or better yet, tell us where the fish are?"

"Good brother, that may be a little too much for the Messiah. I think you're asking for something that only God can do." ∎

MorningStar on Television

The MorningStar Program can now be seen on

TBN Church Channel on **Direct TV**
Thursdays at 9:30 p.m., EST.
If you would like to receive the TBN Church Channel on cable,
please solicit your local cable company.

We can also be seen in Europe, the Middle East, and North Africa on
GOD Revival
Wednesdays at 00:30 a.m. • **Saturdays at 11:30 a.m.**
Sundays at 19:30 p.m.

GOD Channel
Sundays at 2:00 p.m. • **Mondays at 2:00 a.m. and 8:30 a.m.** (UK time)

The programs include live worship as well as speakers and teachers that
we feel have a present word for the church in our times.

MORNINGSTAR WEBSITE
www.morningstarministries.org

Word for the Week From Rick Joyner • Special Bulletins for Current Events • Online Store with Books and Music • Conference Information • Q&A with Rick Joyner • MorningStar School of Ministry Information • MorningStar Fellowships—Charlotte • Wilkesboro • Winston-Salem • Wilmington • MorningStar Subscriptions—Journal • Prophetic Bulletin • Message of the Month • Itineraries ... AND MUCH MORE

[Equipping the Saints for the Work of Ministry]

MorningStar
FELLOWSHIP CHURCH

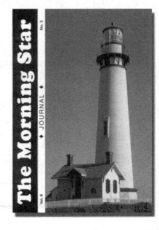

MorningStar
STRATEGIC TEAM
UNIFIED FOR ADVANCEMENT

MST IS:
a unique fellowship of our ministry partners who are united with us in heart and action for our strategic purposes in these times.

MST FINANCES:
are used for the restoration of H.I.M. and missions that equip and send out leaders full of power and love for the advancement of the kingdom of Jesus Christ.

MEMBERS CONTRIBUTE A MINIMUM OF:
$15.^{00} per month or $150.^{00} per year
(but you can give more!)

TO JOIN CONTACT MST AT
1-800-542-0278